The Trees Were Spinning

Erik Black

Published by Erik Black, 2016.

THE TREES WERE SPINNING

First edition. May 19, 2016.

Copyright © 2016 Erik Black.

ISBN: 979-8224844180

Written by Erik Black.

the trees were spinning

by erik black

THE TREES WERE SPINNING
by Erik Black

a memoir of my two years in Kenya
cover photo of baobab tree by the author

Dedication

This book is dedicated to the Duruma people, who always said I would write a book about them, even before I knew I would. I also want to thank Cora and Julie in the monthly writer's group, without whom this work might not have ever been completed. Many thanks to the team I shared so many adventures with: Marv and Jan, David and Julia, Lanny and Carla, Dyanna, Jaclynnette and Corrine, Dave and Shaune, Dean and Heather, Jonathon and Agnes. And last but never least my wonderful wife Deborah who only knows Africa through my (often repeated) stories but listens intently whenever I say, "Have I told you about the time...."

CHAPTERS:

Introduction

<u>By the same Author</u>

Introduction

In Kenya, all the trees can spin, and I think this is true all around the world.

In 1995 my first wife and I joined a team of missionaries to live among a tribe in Kenya, East Africa. Our tribe was called the Duruma, and they spoke both their tribal dialect and a trade language called Swahili. Only a few of them spoke English. The Duruma were considered unreached, meaning they had few if any indigenous churches, and as a whole could not be considered Christian. We went there to plant the seeds of a church and help it to grow in numbers and in spiritual depth.

For a number of years I had felt called to be a missionary. I just knew that Africa was my destination, and after looking into several mission groups that worked in Africa we made our choice. Quitting jobs and selling a few of our few possessions, we said goodbye to family and most things familiar and gave ourselves into the hands of God.

We were part of a two-year program of Africa Inland Mission, or AIM. The program brought together an experienced missionary leader or leaders and several green missionaries. We were the green ones.

The purpose of our two years was to give us instruction, both academic and hands-on, in various aspects of the missionary life. These areas included language learning, cultural adaptation, spiritual warfare, evangelism, and church growth. We studied books on various subjects ranging from anthropology to the history of missions, and then tried to apply what we were learning to our present situation. In this way we could see if a particular theory was well-suited to our people group, or best left in a book on the shelf.

Our team lived in several villages out in the bush about an hour inland from the port city of Mombasa. The Kenyan pastor of our church, as well as the team leaders, lived in a village called Majengo, but my wife and I lived further out in a place named Miyani. At first, the church met under a baobab tree in Majengo, with most of us sitting on the ground. Our first Sunday there, a herd of goats wandered among the congregation, and young boys played soccer nearby.

We lived on donations given by individuals and churches back home in America. Our salary was below the poverty level by Western standards, but upper middle class in Kenya. As hard as we tried to live simply and identify with our neighbors, there would always be a financial gap between us. Sometimes our extra money would bless the families in our church and village, and sometimes it would buy us some sanity in the form of chocolate or a much needed break from the village. Sometimes there was no extra money.

I must confess we were not prepared for life in rural Africa. We went with our ideals, our thoughts of how we could save the world with a few well-crafted sermons and a couple years of our lives. I do not diminish what happened in those two years, but it was different than we expected: less dramatic, less broad-sweeping and grandiose, and more inward and quiet.

To think that God works only in the obvious and the famous is to miss God in our lives. More often than we expect, He appears veiled and hushed, in the still-small voice that leads us down the path a bit farther, always into the unknown.

To think that God works only in missionaries, preachers, and holy men is equally to miss His plan and His ways. Jesus called simple men and shaped them into His church. He is still doing that today. Missionaries are quite normal people, more so than most people realize. They are no more special than anyone else, though their lives might sound quite exciting at times. Read on to see how God took my ordinary life from Missouri to Kenya and back again, and used me and changed me along the way.

A truth that I knew well and still know is this: The ten thousand miles between here and a dusty village in Kenya are nothing compared with the spiritual distance God Almighty is willing to go to reach those He is trying to save. Our sacrifice is worth even one life that is changed for the better.

Chapter 1: Acrobats and Geckos

We lived in a village in Kenya called Miyani which was about 25 kilometers or an hours' drive from the port city of Mombasa and the Indian Ocean. To say ours was the nicest house in our village is mostly true, at least from a Western point of view, though nice is not a word most people would use to describe any house in that village. It was built of cinder-block with a cement floor and a tin roof. The walls were plaster, and below the tin roof was a mud ceiling, which greatly reduced the heat, but also increased the amount of dirt inside the home. The windows all had bars on them, in contrast to the average Duruma house in which most of the windows were closed up with mud. Privacy was highly valued in many African cultures, at least in the home, and there was also a strong mistrust of strangers when it came to personal property.

The front porch faced west and was shaded and had two cement benches, a rare thing which attracted children of all ages at all times of the day or evening. A large oakish-looking tree grew in the front "yard", which was itself nothing but packed-down dirt. These dirt yards were easy enough to keep clean, being swept every morning by a family member bent over a handmade grass broom. The house had been built originally as a *duka,* or small store, which was why it had the benches out front. Our landlord Muhammad Badi lived next door in a similar house with the younger of his two wives.

Inside the house there was a large living room, with our woven-stick chairs providing sturdy though uncomfortable seating. On the north side was the front bedroom, which quickly became the infrequent guest room due to the aforementioned children sitting and talking on the front porch. Through a hallway was the "master" bedroom, which by some grace of God was never plagued by creepy crawlies like snakes, mice, or scorpions (that we knew of) that were prevalent in the rest of the house. Across the hall was our kitchen with a small window into the living room, convenient for serving food. At the end of the hall there was a doorway into the back part of the house, partly open to the sky. Around the corner was the back door (seldom used), and again on the north side was a third "bedroom" that we used as a storage room for leftover building materials and odd supplies.

Across from this room, in the southeast corner, was our bathroom, called a *cho* in Swahili. It was nearly unheard of among the villagers to have a bathroom, and especially a toilet, inside the house or directly connected to it. This was due to the belief that evil spirits inhabited unclean places, both a traditional and an Islamic belief. But we, being Westerners, had insisted on having an inside toilet and bathroom, both for privacy and convenience.

It was this path to the bathroom, especially at night, which caused us quite a lot of anxiety the first few months. As there was no electricity, every trip to the *cho* required the use of a flashlight or a kerosene lantern held in one hand. Being in rural Kenya, one always had to be alert where one stepped to avoid snakes, spiders, scorpions, centipedes, mice, or otherwise harmless but crunchy bugs. But additionally the trip to the *cho* required us to look up as well, for always there were one or two bats that preferred the back hallway to roost instead of under the tin roof. Before we had our "system" down, going to the *cho* involved running like headless chickens when the light disturbed the bat, who would flutter and fly about us. His name was Wayne, as in Bruce Wayne, the alter ego of Batman. Once we learned about Wayne, we developed a trick to avoid him. When we opened the door to the back part of the house at night, we would shine a light on Wayne, who would stir and then fly off into the night, allowing us to go about our business in peace. That worked quite well for the duration of our two years in the village. The problem was that Wayne had a girlfriend. We named her Wendy, short for *wendaphi* which means, "Where are you going?" in the Duruma language. Wendy seemed to have a faulty radar system, so instead of just flying away when the light was shone on her, she would do crazy circles around us, forcing us to duck and run as if we were in a war zone. A couple of times she even flew into my chest.

In addition to our two acrobats, we had tan house geckos on the walls. The geckos had names as well because, so the theory goes, if you can name something you have power over it and the fear diminishes. All of the geckos were named Frank. Some of them were given the nickname "FF" for Frank's Friend, if they looked different enough from the normal gecko. Frank was a friend indeed, as both geckos and the bats ate lots of mosquitoes for us (I never did enjoy eating the mosquitoes, and somebody sure needed to).

The house gecko is an amazing creature. The body is partly translucent, and the skeleton (and lunch) could be seen if the gecko was on a window screen. Their toes had multiple suctions called lamellae for clinging to any surface, even moving quite fast. When they met another gecko, they would both squeak and chatter much like miniature squirrels, and chase each other until one gave up the territory. Unfortunately, the Duruma had a primal fear of all lizards, and geckos and others would often be seen smacked with a broom and swept out of the house. Meanwhile the flies and mosquitoes flourished. In any culture, man and nature are out of balance one way or another.

We got used to the critters living in and around our house. That's not to say we didn't overreact sometimes. Mice always did my wife in, but the foot-long centipedes with orange or blue legs creeped me out the most. The neighbors probably got quite a kick out of hearing our screams and reactions to unwanted guests, and since no real harm ever came from any of the critters, it all added to the vividness of our experience in Kenya.

Our house had a great view over the valley to the west, filled with *shambas* (farms) of maize and coconuts. Behind us to the east was the *kaya,* a wooded hill sacred to the Duruma tribe, and to the northeast was Mombasa harbor, where we could dimly see the ships out on the Indian Ocean. The sunsets always amazed us, as did the starry night sky, vastly different from our accustomed view in Missouri, including a showing of the Southern Cross. Africa was so full of life, sometimes quite primal, yet always near; a land caught between earth and sky, between life and death. Everyone we know who has spent any time there feels that the experience gets into your blood and changes you forever. Our little house on the hill with the pleasant sea breeze was full of memory and experience and life. We went there to change the Duruma; it was we who were changed.

CHAPTER 2: MIMI?

"My wife, *Mimi,* has gone to town for the day."

Our neighbor Mohammed, informed me casually about the day's events. I barely noticed the slight emphasis in his voice when he mentioned her name. So much was still so new, and some is still new even now as I write this.

My wife had learned in the first few days the Swahili phrase to ask a name, and had used it right away on the neighbors.

"What are you called?" "Mimi!?" had been the clear response, and she then told her name to the woman.

Some names were easier for us Westerners to remember and pronounce than others. Mohammed, Beja, and Hudumu I remembered quickly, while Chilwengi, Tsaum, and Ngombe took a while longer. Likely they had as much trouble with our names, but there were just the two of us living on the hill, and we were meeting dozens of people in a village of several hundred.

The Wa-Duruma, as they call themselves, are a people who honor their guests almost above family status. When a guest arrives at their home, whether he is expected or not, a chicken will be killed and cooked if there is one and the best seat (sometimes only marginally more comfortable than going without) will be offered. The foreigner has a near-permanent status as a guest; that is, as a white man in a black nation I will never be mistaken for a family member, so they can consider me a family member without offending the rest of the family or corrupting their blood-lines.

The foreigner was deferred to in knowledge and opinion. Whether they really believed it or not, they would often tell us we were smarter and more sophisticated than they were. We would argue that people are just different all over the world, none of us better than another, but they would respond that Westerners have better technology and a higher standard of living, so they are smarter than the Africans. At the least, we did not assume that proud opinion of ourselves, and worked to affirm the Duruma's esteem of themselves. I think that they had lived so long under the authority of others, especially as a British colony, that they assumed that was the way of things. That being said, there was a spirit of pride in themselves, an identity that revealed itself over time. It was the quiet listening to how to "improve" their lives in one way or another, and then continuing to do things the way they had been done for centuries. If we had come in as teachers of a better way of life, we would have left frustrated after our two years there, broken by the stubborn land and the people we came to change. But we came in as learners—learners of language, culture, cooking, living and life. That made much difference in our experience, as well as opening up a few opportunities for us to teach as well.

Coming as missionaries, we had studied anthropology a bit, along with various evangelistic approaches. We knew the mistakes that some in the past had made in wanting to do things only in a Western way, and essentially forming a Western Church when they had any success at all. We were determined to encourage an indigenous church that had its own style of worship and way of doing things. The songs we enjoyed were the ones they had created themselves and were almost always in Chi-Duruma, rather than the Western hymns translated into Swahili that never sounded quite right (but maybe that was just our presumption that again we knew what all their songs should sound like).

When we met a few local Christians for the first time they immediately told us, "We're glad you are here. Now you can do the work of evangelism for us, since you know how better than we do." Our response, which seemed to be accepted a bit, was not only that they knew their language and culture intimately, but that they also had many family and social contacts that we would never have, and so they were much better suited to doing the work of the Lord than we were. We were there to come alongside them and encourage them, but not to in any way supplant them.

The guest was always right, even when he was wrong. Not that anyone would have changed the course of his life for the sake of the guest, but there were quite a few small accommodations for us during our time.

A couple of weeks after learning the name of our neighbor's younger wife, and calling her by that name, and her responding to it, and her husband using that name to refer to her, we began to learn that *Mimi* wasn't really her name.

My wife had been amazed that so many of the women in our village were named *Mimi*. Then as we learned more language, we realized that "*mimi*" means "me," and when you asked someone, "What's your name?" they respond with, "Who me?" and then you say, "Yes you!" and they tell you their name. We were only halfway there.

We had quite a laugh at ourselves, the first of many language laughs that would involve both Chi-Duruma and English, like hearing the children roll their "r" in the word "armpit." What got us through the challenge of language learning was our attitude of being learners rather than teachers, being there to serve rather than to lead. And a good sense of humor.

CHAPTER 3: Chiguba, Mambo and Me

During my two years in Kenya, I acquired three different names. This was in addition to the cries of *"M'zungu! M'zungu!"* (meaning "white person") which the children would call out when I entered a village where people did not know me.

A week or so after we arrived, our team decided we all would do a home stay, where we would each stay in a Duruma home for three or four days and nights. Several families in the new church offered to have a couple stay with them, and would be given some money to cover the cost of feeding us. It would be an excellent opportunity for a cultural exchange and for us to learn the language and customs from an insider's view.

Hudumu was a man in the church I took a liking to. Maybe it was his smile or friendly nature, or just that his name reminded me somehow of Harry Houdini. So it was decided that my wife and I would stay with Hudumu and his wife, Mbeyu, and their four kids in their village of Chingoluni. Their home was a 10-minute walk from the main village of Majengo where the church was, but a full hour from our home in Miyani.

We brought bedding and a mosquito net, and they gave us their room to sleep in. The days were enjoyable and challenging, with everything still so new and our language ability less than a toddler. But the nights were not so restful. Maybe it was the bats that slept directly above us, the lack of privacy or knowing we had displaced our hosts out of their own bed. Maybe it was the immersion in everything strange, but I think it was the mouse that summed it up for me.

The first night I forgot to tuck in the mosquito net. It was sufficient for keeping most of the nasties away from us, but not all. In the middle of the night I woke with a start, realizing a mouse was crawling on me. I smacked it off and did a better job with the mosquito net, but the commotion woke my wife. Now, she could handle a lot of creepy things, but mice were one of her top fears. So when she asked me, "Why did you wake up so suddenly?" I could only answer,

"It was nothing, go back to sleep." Only when we were "safely" back in our own home did I tell her about the rodent.

My wife spent her days on the home stay working with Mbeyu and other women of her village: pounding corn, carrying buckets of water up a steep gorge from the river below, cooking, cleaning, and looking after kids. My days were spent sitting on a hard wooden chair, talking with Hudumu and his brother (much more listening than talking for me), and looking out over the valley behind their village compound. I had no idea why, but my remarks about the hardness of the chairs seemed to fall on deaf ears with my wife. At least the other men on our team agreed with me when we talked at church the next week.

Toward the end of the home stay, Hudumu told me I would be called *Mambo* in his village, after his brother. In the Duruma language, *mambo* meant "talk" or "words," but it was also used as a casual greeting, to which the listener would respond with *safi*, meaning "fine." The slang translation might be something like, "What's the word?" "Fine!" So ever after when someone from Hudumu's village greeted me as Mambo, I would respond, "*Safi!*"

When we returned to our home village of Miyani, our landlord Mohammed told me, "You can't be called Mambo in our village, because you are part of our family and clan, and Mambo is a name from another clan. We must give you a new name. We will call you *Chiguba*."

The Duruma tribe was divided into fourteen clans, seven patriarchal and seven which were matriarchal. A man could only marry a woman from a different clan, as clans were very much extended families. I have long forgotten the name of our clan, but not the families in it.

A person's clan was known by his or her name, though a few names were common to all. Some names were for everyday things like corn, cows, weeds, seed, and sun. When Mohammed gave me the name of Chiguba, I asked him what it meant. He said it didn't have a meaning that he knew of. I always suspected that it meant "big dumb ugly white guy who looks funny and smells worse." No one would ever confirm that meaning for me, though.

So wherever I went, people knew me as Chiguba or more fully Chiguba wa Badi, meaning I was the son of Badi, which was Mohammed's tribal name. When a Duruma person met another for the first time, they would trace their families back until they knew each other's relatives. In this way they could determine whether the new person was from a good family or not, and whether they would be friends. Our landlord Mohammed Badi was a respected older man, or *mzee*, so that was good for us as well. And I secretly thought he also gained some renown for renting us his second house.

It was on one of his introductory tours that I received my third name. We were sitting eating *ugali* with a family we had just met. The father, on hearing that I had been given a Duruma name, decided in his house I would be called Tom Mazera, or Tom Corn. The name never stuck, and that was the only day I was called that.

My wife was named *Nadzuwa*, which meant "like the sun," and was also the name of one of Hudumu and Mbeyu's daughters. That name she kept for the whole two years. The reason she got to keep her name was that Mohammed assumed I would have married someone from another clan, and so it was accepted. I never met another Chiguba, which could either be a mark of distinction or a mark of near extinction.

Having Duruma names meant we belonged, at least as much as we could with our very white skin and our poor language skills and strange culinary preferences. Wherever I went I was introduced as Chiguba, and this is how I introduced myself as well. I treasured my name, and hearing it still brings back all of the memories. That name is a key into a life I once lived, a way to touch that place and be with those people again. It is as much a part of my own identity as my birth name, and I will carry it all my days.

CHAPTER 4: The Unclothing of the Wazungu

I imagined Africa as a dangerous place where all sorts of deadly creatures thrived and I would be walking through fields with snakes growing like grass, swaying in the slight breeze. Naturally I packed protective clothing. I told myself that I needed durable but modest clothes, long khaki pants and good leather hiking boots, so I would be respected as well as comfortable. But the little thought behind my purchases was, "How can I keep the creepy crawlies away from my body?"

In hot weather, my normal choice in clothing would be sandals, shorts and T-shirts. This, we were told, was not what adults wore among the Duruma tribe. I brought my comfortable clothes to wear on vacation, but brought more modest clothing for the village, including long pants and button-down shirts.

"How much did your boots cost? I bet they were almost 1200 shillings [$60 at that time]." We were having tea with the family of someone in the local church. I looked down at my fancy Vasque waterproof breathable boots with a price tag of $180 and nodded, "Yeah, you're about right." I was embarrassed at the cost, which was far more than an average family made in a month. I had come prepared for all of the elements except the human one.

Traditional Duruma men wore a garment called a *kikoi*. This was a colorful piece of thin fabric sewn together end to end to form a tube. The man stepped into this tube and then tied it tight around his waist. I consider this no more than a manly skirt. Even more modern men would often wear the *kikoi* in the morning or evening. I never got used to wearing them, though they were comfortable and cooler than pants in hot weather. I could never shake the thought that I was wearing a skirt.

For men, and definitely women, exposing the leg much above the knee was very immodest and never done. Hence the reason for wearing long pants.

Another factor in deciding what to wear is the cultural standard of saving the best clothes for visiting friends and family in other villages or going on any kind of journey. Around the house, any old rags could be worn unless the family was expecting guests.

Children often had only one nice outfit which was saved for special days, and another outfit that was worn to threads day after day. School age children had to wear the school uniform during the week. Miyani Primary School students wore green shorts or skirts and a yellow button down shirt, purchased or tailored locally. Most kids had only one school uniform which was washed every day or two.

Women wore a traditional cloth called a *kanga*. This was bought as a double-length piece of thin fabric which was cut and hemmed by a tailor, working at a pedal-powered sewing machine. They were printed in Mombasa with traditional proverbs and sayings, some familiar and some that made no sense to our Western minds. These were in Swahili, the trade language of East Africa used by all fifty-some tribes in Kenya. One *kanga* was wrapped around a woman's waist and tucked in to form a skirt. The other matching piece was used either as a headscarf or as a sling to carry a baby on her back. Often two friends would each wear one of the pieces to show their connected lives. The *kanga* could also be rolled up and used as a cushion when she was carrying a 20-gallon water bucket on her head (sometimes at the same time as a baby on her back). A woman would have several *kangas* and would use the worn out fabric as a towel when bathing her children. A versatile and long-lived piece of clothing!

I noticed a progression (or should I say digression) in my clothing during the first month or two in the village. The first thing to change was my boots. Though they were waterproof and bugproof and snakeproof, they were also heavy and warm. After three weeks of walking the trails and seeing no snakes, the boots were stowed in a trunk only to be used once when I climbed Mount Kilimanjaro on a vacation. In their place I wore Teva sandals, and later simply flip flops that could be purchased for about fifty cents and lasted a long time. The only disadvantage to the flip flops was in the rainy season when they would get stuck in the mud while walking. At these times I sometimes resorted to going barefoot, even with all I had read about ringworms, hookworms, pinworms and the like. But I never went barefoot around the house, on account of the scorpions which came out in the rainy season.

I continued to wear pants whenever I left the village, but again after a month or two I wore mostly shorts when I was near my home. Nice button-down shirts were reserved for church and town days, and at home I wore T-shirts. So comfort won out over style and even modesty, as all things fade under the scorching African sun. Looking back, I should have reserved shorts for vacations only since adults did not wear them, but sometimes in survival mode a person can think of only making it through another hot and dusty day.

Clothing given to charity in America sometimes made its way to Africa, usually not so charitable after the long voyage but sold for a profit. Since Africans had different styles than Americans, and different ideas of modesty, we would sometimes see rather odd combinations of clothing. My fondest memory of this was a man in the church named Julius Tsuma. Julius was a stout man, having worked as a bouncer at a dance club in Mombasa for several years before moving back to the village. One Sunday we were having lunch with his family after church and he was showing us some pictures of him when he was younger. In one picture, Julius was wearing stirrup pants, with the loops proudly not tucked under his feet. We asked him why he was wearing women's clothing. His answer: "Pants are for men, because women don't wear pants!"

Tourist t-shirts are bought in America as souvenirs, given to children to placate them when Grandma comes back from her cruise. When we are bored with last year's vacation shirt, we get a new one and donate the old shirt. And all the donated shirts in the world eventually end up in Africa. Well, almost all. In rural Kenya, t-shirts were worn simply as coverings and not for what was written on them. Not too many people spoke English, and fewer still could read our language. In our village alone, we observed a number of odd sayings on t-shirts worn by both men and women. One of Beja's wives frequently wore a red shirt that proudly said, "I rode the Wisconsin Duck!" Another woman's shirt said, "Marge is 40," though whoever Marge was I never knew, not exactly a local name. My personal favorite was a man wearing a shirt that said, "One in the oven" with an arrow pointing down to his belly. Then again, maybe he did know what it meant....

When we left, we took few clothes with us. Some had expired along the way, and the rest felt like they belonged with our poorer Kenyan friends rather than being extra baggage to bring home. Just before we left the village for the last time, I took a box of clothing to the group of houses below us, and left the box in the middle of the village compound. It nearly started a riot.

I had brought one thing that was very out of place in the village, but was a prized possession for that very reason: A pair of Converse high tops. These I wore only when I went into town, to feel a bit more American perhaps. My neighbor's teenage son Fujo took a liking to them, and often asked to borrow them for special times. When I returned home to America, I left those shoes with Fujo. Though they are undoubtedly worn out to threadbare, I still imagine him walking on some dusty trail, wearing my pair of purple high tops.

CHAPTER 5: MENENGALA AND THE MANGO BANK

There are three and only three kinds of trees that are cultivated by the Duruma, and in fact most of the tribes on the coast of Kenya. Every other tree is either an accidental that is left for shade, or a medicinal tree like the *neem*, whose leaves and bark are used to treat malaria among other ailments. Goats often break the branches down to eat the leaves of the *neem*, perhaps to cure a stomach ache (from eating too much garbage).

The most important tree is the coconut palm. Coconut milk is used in cooking, young coconuts provide a refreshing drink on a hot day, the palms are woven together for roofing material, mats, baskets, and even doors, and the empty halves of the coconut shell are made into ladles or tools. So important are coconut trees that the trees themselves are often sold separately from the land they grow on, and deeded from father to son.

Next are the cashew trees. Cashew nuts are harvested and then sold in Mombassa, or simply roasted to remove the poisonous hull and sold in the village to those who don't have any cashew trees. There was a large factory for processing cashews on the way into Mombassa, and sometimes the black smoke covered the highway so that travelers had to hold their breath while driving through the toxic fumes.

Last are the mango trees. The best varieties are planted in the fertile valleys; that fruit is sold in town and seldom eaten in the village. These look much like the rather expensive fruit that can be bought at most supermarkets in the West. The taste is far superior in Kenya, because time and travel are the enemies of fresh produce.

But there are wild mango trees that no one claims as their own. The fruit is smaller and the flavor is not as rich as the mangoes sold in the city. These are used in cooking sometimes, to impart a lemony-sour taste. To be honest, I seldom ever saw a ripe mango, because the children would have picked the tree clean long before a fruit could have a chance to ripen completely. They harvest them by throwing sticks into the branches above them (not the safest or most efficient means, but a lot of fun). Then being quite under-ripe and hard, the kids would beat them to a pulp against a hard surface and proceed to suck out whatever juice was inside. I never quite took to eating green mangos, preferring fruit that was a bit riper. To each their own.

"Hodi!" came the call at the screen door, the universal greeting from one outside the house to anyone inside. We answered the door to find Menengala, the 7-year old daughter of our neighbor Mohammed and his younger wife Mwanajuma (formerly known as Mimi). Her arms were filled with green mangos harvested from the tree in the field out front.

Now, being a culture that values the community and the family over the individual, nothing is ever really kept for only one person. Clothes are shared in the family, food is shared with neighbors, and anything resembling a toy is shared among the children. Any good thing you have must be shared with your family, especially younger children. And if someone asks you for something and you have it, you are supposed to give it, though there are ways to avoid giving up something you need or want for yourself. Mostly you hide what you have, so others won't even know to ask for it.

When we went to town once a week to stock up on groceries, we always bought extra things for our neighbors. Tomatoes were hard to get in the village, so we usually bought an extra kilo or two for different families, along with some other items frequently asked for. When we had given away the extra tomatoes, we would simply tell the neighbor that we didn't have any more, which in their culture can mean we didn't have any more to give. But it never hurts to ask again.

Our neighbor's daughter Menengala knew the cultural mores, the responsibility for her younger siblings, the sharing that must go on. And she did her part well, carrying the baby on her back, helping cook and clean, and running errands for her family. She was a good Duruma girl. Mostly.

When Menengala brought the mangos, I thanked her and wondered what we were going to do with so many green tart fruits. So when she returned after half an hour and asked for one of the mangos, I gladly gave it to her. And then in another 20 minutes she came and asked for another mango, which I gave to her. Then another, and another, until most of the mangos were gone, returned to the child who had brought them to us.

It was then I realized what was going on. Menengala, in order to get around the cultural norm of sharing, was keeping her mangos out of sight from the other children and enjoying them one by one. If she only had one at a time, she could get away with not sharing it with others and so enjoy the whole pile all by herself. We were her mango bank. And she was a very clever girl!

CHAPTER 6: RIDING THE GREEN BEAST

The Beast broke down again. The Beast had a flat tire. The Beast slid off the road. The Beast, our burden and our lifeline.

Our team consisted of one couple who were the leaders, three "green" couples, and two single women. We each lived in different villages, anywhere from ten minutes to an hour away from the leader's house and the church (initially just a few chairs under a *baobab* tree). Our house was the lucky one with an hour's walk to get to church or team meetings.

We shared one vehicle between all of us, a green diesel Toyota Landcruiser, already old and beat up by the time we arrived on the scene to beat it up some more. The Beast, as we called it, was quite solid, made for driving on the rough dry dirt roads in the bush, and the even worse wet and muddy roads. We mainly used it for the once-a-week trips into Mombassa to stock up on whatever couldn't be bought locally, to pick up our mail, and to eat at one of several restaurants (our favorite we named "Dive Number Two"). Near the end of our time in Kenya we replaced the Beast with a white van, only slightly more reliable.

The Beast had a full back seat, and a pickup bed covered with a cage that could be locked. The ten of us on the team could not fit in the main riding area, and the men would ride in the back if we were all going somewhere (which wasn't often, considering the dust and lack of comfort in the back). Going into Mombassa, usually only half of the team traveled on any one trip. Even then, with extra Duruma passengers, some of us would ride in the back, a mix of Americans and Africans equally uncomfortable with the journey.

None of us liked having the Beast parked at our house, for two reasons. The first was that even though it was a team vehicle, having it at our house was a status symbol we didn't really want. We tried hard to fit in with the

Duruma and to minimize the many differences between us. Having the green Beast seemed like a visible flaunting of our wealth and a reminder that we never would fit in, try as we might.

The second reason we hated having the vehicle at our house (and everyone else did too) involved a request from the chief of the Duruma in our area before most of the team had arrived. There was a great need to help sick people get to a hospital, either in Mombassa or to another town called Kinango which was slightly closer but all dirt road to get there. There was also a need to bring back the body of a person who had died at the hospital so they could be buried in the village near their family. Hospital runs and body runs we called them. For hospital runs, we charged a nominal fee that didn't come close to covering the cost of fuel but merely helped the Duruma feel it wasn't charity. For the body runs, we charged the full cost of going to town and coming back since it was less of an emergency crisis that a family was in. This was still less than half what the local transports charged to bring a body to the village. A number of team discussions were wasted on how much we should charge if we take a sick person to the hospital but then they died and we brought them back on the same trip.

The Duruma were a strong people, not used to crying over pain (women were even instructed not to cry out during childbirth, so as not to scare other women from having children). They would come to our house asking for a Band-Aid to hold together a gaping wound that needed stitches, or for a little ointment to heal an infection they had carried for weeks or even months. This toughness, along with an extreme sense of frugality, meant they seldom would go to the doctor unless the person was nearly dying. Somehow this always came to a crux at night.

So whichever house the vehicle was parked at (and the villagers somehow always knew) would receive an urgent *hodi* late at night. Then the man of the house would drive the sick person and a few family members to the hospital, sometimes waiting there for quite a while to ensure that a doctor was actually going to see the person, and then return to the village. During the night drives, my main thought was not to get a flat tire or have a breakdown. I never did, but it was always the thing that worried me the most far from any street lights or tow trucks.

Body runs were thankfully less frequent. I only drove one the entire two years in the village, but it was a memory I will never forget.

The morgue in Mombassa was subject to the same rolling power outages that the whole country endured regularly (for those that had the luxury of electricity anyways). Bodies that should have been kept at a constant temperature near freezing were subject to regular fluctuations. As I approached the morgue, my nose began to burn with the intensity of the stench, and I wrinkled my forehead in pain. I wondered how anyone could stand to live anywhere near that place. When we arrived, we discovered that the morgue was closed for a while during the middle of the day, but the people told us it would be open "very soon" and we should just wait there. Very soon lasted about an hour. The body was wrapped in plastic I had brought to keep the back of our vehicle cleaner. A number of men from the family had come to escort the body back to her village for a proper burial. Most of them rode in the back with the body. When we were within sight of the family's home, the women of the village as if on cue began to wail in their fashion. Thus the remains of their beloved were brought home and laid to rest in the family plot.

The Beast served us and the Duruma well. The times I hated driving the most, other than hospital or body runs, were during the rainy season. The roads from the village were made of packed clay and gravel, but mostly clay. When it rained, the entire driving surface (along with every path you could walk on) turned into slippery, sticky red-brown clay. Driving was a nightmare. Uphill was worse, because it was nearly impossible to get any traction on the road. Often we would unload all the passengers and the men would push the thing most of the way uphill. Then we would all embark, and slip down the other side, hoping to avoid sliding into the ditch or slamming into a tree. The road had huge gullies carved into it from torrential rainwater that didn't have time to soak into the ground. It was often more pleasant to walk in the mud than to ride the bumpy road.

I remember one time when it was my turn to drive into town. It wasn't raining that morning, but it had been for several days before. Few of the women on our team had a license to drive in Kenya, and at these times I envied them. For me there was the tension between not wanting to get the car stuck and look like a fool, and not wanting to ask someone else to drive for me and look like a fool. So a fool I was. My wife asked me, "Do you want Dean to drive instead?" I responded, "I can get this thing stuck as easy as anyone else!" And I did.

CHAPTER 7: The Three Little Goats (a good story that went wrong)

" *Once long ago, there were three little…*Hey, how do you say 'pigs' in Chi-Duruma? Oh, the Duruma don't like pigs. I'll say 'goats' instead."

"Once long ago, there were three little goats who said goodbye to their mother and went out into the world to build houses of their own."

We were sitting on the neighbor's porch (his and ours being the only two porches in the village) after a not-so-inspiring dinner of *ugali* and greens, the Kenyan staple meal made with cornmeal. It was a cooler night, with the breeze from the sea making the flying insects work harder to bite us. All of their children had been bathed and dressed for bed, wrapped in *kangas*—the multi-purpose cloths used alternatively for a wraparound skirt, a head covering, a sling for babies to be carried on their mother's backs, or something to tie up a bundle of corn to be taken to the mill for grinding.

We were exchanging fairy tales and stories with Muhammad and his two wives and children. So much can be learned about a culture by hearing their stories. Even as our stories often have a moral at the end, so theirs also revealed insights into what they valued in life, and their hopes and fears, though often without a moral at the end to summarize the message.

Many of the Duruma traditional tales involved magic and jealousy, and often the meaning gets lost in translation. One of the more straightforward stories we heard explains why the chicken (*kuku*) scratches the ground and the falcon (*phanga*) steals chicks to eat.

Long ago the chicken and the falcon were friends. They used to eat together and help each other in times of need. One day the chicken asked to borrow a knife from the falcon to cut her children's hair. The falcon warned her not to lose the knife, or he would begin stealing the baby chicks to eat. Very soon the foolish chicken did lose the knife, and she searched for it everywhere by scratching the ground. And so the falcon swoops from the sky and steals her chicks to this day.

"The first little goat was lazy. He found some grass and made it into a house to live in, and played the day away."

After I said this, I looked down the hill at Muhammad's outdoor kitchen and corn crib, which was a traditional Duruma grass house. The frame was wood poles lashed together, but over this it was completely covered in thatch. The roof literally touched the ground, making the house look like one enormous haystack. The grass was hand cut with a sickle by the women, and carried on their heads great distances over a period of days or weeks until they had gathered enough. Then the husband would tie the grass together and form the house, leaving a very small hole in the roof to let out the smoke from the cooking fire. The whole process was anything but lazy, and in fact was quite resourceful using local materials and knowledge.

"Actually, he wasn't lazy; he just didn't have the time for making a stronger house." My feeble attempt at backpedaling weakened my story, and flustered me somewhat. As the neighbors didn't seem to be offended in any way (not that they would have shown that to me), I resumed my storytelling.

"The second little goat was smarter and built his house out of sticks, and he was happy."

The "modern" Duruma house is built of sticks – small tree poles lashed together into a rectangle frame, and smaller poles filling the space in between. Then thick clay-mud is packed into the frame layer upon layer to build the walls, which afforded some cooling effect to the inside of the house. Finally, the roof was made of *makuti,* which was coconut palm branches woven together to make (nearly) rainproof shingles. The *makuti* would need to be replaced every few years, and the clay in the walls as well, but as these materials were easily acquired, it was quite an economical and sustainable house.

"The third little goat built his house out of cinderblocks and cement, because he wanted a strong and long-lasting house that would not fall down when the rains came."

Even as I said this, I looked over at our rented house and at Muhammad's, which was much the same style. Cement floors, cinderblock and plaster walls, tin roof. Very long-lasting and low maintenance, if one could afford it. Ours were the only two in the village, out of hundreds of traditional houses. Even with our house being the nicest in the village, it was still quite a few steps down from anywhere we had lived in America. My own mother's first reaction when she saw a picture of our Duruma house was that it needed to be condemned and bulldozed. Maybe she was right, at least by our high standards in the West. The back part of the house was starting to fall away, and we had enough wildlife living in the floors, walls, and ceilings to start our own exotic zoo. But still, it was quite nice in comparison, and sometimes a little perspective is all you need to encourage contentment with what you have.

"The hyena came and blew down the house made of grass, and he blew down the house made of sticks, but he couldn't blow down the house made of cinderblocks. So the goats ate him and lived happily ever after."

I wished I had chosen a different Western story to tell my neighbors, but maybe most of our stories would somehow come out wrong when told in another language and to people with a very different worldview. Think of "Cinderella" or "The Ugly Duckling" or "Snow White" and what these stories illustrate about our culture and what we value the most in life. Money, power, appearance and status are things we seek as a culture, and these will often come into our tales. Perhaps it is we who need to hear new stories, to be changed in our thinking and our value system, to become like little children and enter the kingdom of heaven as if for the first time....

CHAPTER 8: TRASHY TOYS

"Chiguba, you can't throw this away! It's a toy!"

Menzole, the ten-year old daughter of our neighbor Muhammad, spoke these words to me as I was burning our trash at the back of our house. Where two full bags of trash per family each week would be normal in America, a Kenyan family might produce 2 bags a year. Trash was burned to reduce the clutter, though by the time the chickens and goats got through the pile there was little left to be burned. And then there were the neighborhood kids.

Whenever anything, including trash, left our house (or for that matter, when anything came into the house) the kids would know about it. They watched us, they knew our patterns and habits and preferences. And though they were good kids for the most part, they were also opportunists, most of all when it came to candy and toys.

Candy was a very rare treat in the village, in contrast to our Western view of dessert after each meal. It was certainly not an essential, and in a society that lived so close to poverty and deprivation, treats were actually treats for them. In Kenya, one could still buy "penny candy", though the taste was rather flat. Even this was not a common purchase for every child.

All candy was called *peramende*, which was probably a corruption of our word peppermint. Children we didn't know well or see often would ask for *peramende* or for shillings, the currency of Kenya. We suspected that the phrase, "Give me five shillings," was the first to be learned in school, since every child knew it. Most of the time we would not give money to children since it perpetuated the begging mentality and was considered extremely rude in their society, much as it would be in ours. But we did give sweets from time to time, mostly to those nearest to our home and known by us.

Friends in the States sent us a box of peppermint candies to give to the village kids. Since giving the whole box out at one time would have caused a stampede of children, we decided to dole them out over a period of weeks. The children next door realized we must have quite the stash of *"peramende"*, and began asking to do chores for us to earn extra sweets. Menzole offered to sweep the "front yard" and Menengala wanted to sweep out the chicken coop (an extra piece of candy for that job). But after a week or so they found other activities to do and forgot about the candy, and so did I. Soon enough the remaining peppermint candies had melted together into a glob of goo in the Equatorial heat and had to be burned at night to avoid the scorn of the children.

Most children did not have toys, at least not as we would know them. They played games like hopscotch, jump rope, and checkers (played with soda bottle caps). They played make-believe, which was mostly role playing what their parents did in the garden or kitchen. In fact, most children had their own chores from a very young age: sweeping, cooking, carrying water and firewood, gathering greens, herding animals, weeding the garden, and taking care of younger siblings. A girl of five might carry her infant brother in a sling on her back, and watch him for an hour or more while the mother worked or went to the store.

The toys kids did have to play with were homemade or scavenged from the trash pile of a richer neighbor. Anything from the big city was especially prized. So when I set out to burn the trash containing a tuna fish can, Menzole scolded me for burning a perfectly good toy: "Chiguba, you can't throw this away! It's a toy!" She grabbed the blackened can with her bare hands to save it from the fire. It would last a few days, maybe a week, as a wheel on an imaginary car or part of another creation. Then discarded again, it might finally come to rest, beyond any possible human use. I ultimately learned to set aside potential play things for the children while I burned that which the Duruma also would burn.

Children throughout the world play football, what we in America call soccer. Kenya is no exception, and kids there (mostly boys) learn early how to kick and move the ball with great skill. The only problem is that even a cheap ball is way beyond the price for a toy in the village, costing a family perhaps most of the month's income. A child could dream, but might not ever play with a real ball. Instead he learned to wrap plastic bags into a makeshift ball using more plastic bags to tightly hold it together, or homemade sisal twine. These balls lacked the spin and distance of a real ball, but they were free and easily repaired when they inevitably came unraveled. They had the added advantage of not going flat when punctured by the ubiquitous thorn.

The best toys were made by fathers with a bit of skill. Sticks and twine, along with four plastic detergent lids, were fashioned together to make a car, complete with a steering wheel attached by a long stick. Then the proud child would race through the village with his car, making all the sounds that any boy in the world can make to escape reality. Even these toys were shared among friends, and unfortunately they did not last too long on the dusty rocky ground. But for a few hours or a few days of play, of joy, it was worth it. As the earth and sky met on the horizon, so the mundane and the heavenly met in a child at play.

CHAPTER 9: SPINNING TREES

Menzole was just under ten years old when we arrived in the village. Her younger sisters, the twins Kashi and Mejumaa, were about seven years old at that time. Few among the Duruma knew exactly how old they were, as it was not a concern of their daily lives. Birth records were not always kept, though this habit was changing as the modern world encroached upon them.

The twins and Menzole all lived with their mother, Nzingo, who was the elder wife of our neighbor and landlord, Muhammad Badi. Initially Nzingo and her girls did not live next door to us with the younger wife, Mwanajuma, but at Muhammad's "country home" at En Gedi, a distance of over an hour away on foot further inland.

We first visited the country home after we had lived in the village for a few weeks. Muhammad was eager to introduce us to the rest of his family and secure his position as tour guide and teacher to the new foreigners. On the way we saw a baboon, and were told that elephants and giraffes could sometimes be seen. Many trees and uncultivated plants grew in that area, and I wondered if some of the land was owned by anyone at all.

When we arrived, the girls came out to meet us on the path and took the things we were carrying (a Duruma tradition of hospitality). The view from there was even better than from our home in Miyani. It was country in the Kenya style, wild among the wild. There was an abundance of trees and shrubs, with many different birds adding their colors to the view. No wonder Muhammad preferred his country home to the village home.

Muhammad killed a chicken for lunch, to honor us as his guests, and as I watched him I thought that I could do that someday. An old neighbor was invited to eat with us. Muhammad told us with a grin, "He doesn't have enough teeth to eat meat. He will only take one piece and suck on it for the rest of the meal." I wondered if that was the reason the old man was invited for lunch.

Indeed the man seemed happy enough to be included at the meal, though I didn't notice how much he ate.

When we left, we asked if we could take a picture of Nzingo and her girls which we would give to them later. This made the twins cry, as their first meeting with white people and a camera all in one day was too much. With gentle words of *"basi, basi"* (enough, enough), their mother tried in vain to console them. Later in our stay they would be hams for the camera with all the other village kids, crying *"Piga piksha, mzungu!"* (Take a picture, white person!).

It was several months later that Muhammad made the decision to move Nzingo and her kids to live in the house next to us. He said that safety was the main reason, as well as having all his kids able to attend school. He had been sharing his time between two houses and two wives. "A house divided cannot stand" but a house with two wives in it will also have its share of troubles. The noise level increased quite a bit, as well as the tension between the two wives. The children seemed to all get along just fine, though. For the most part we enjoyed having the complete family live next door.

Menzole was probably the nicest child in the village. She never seemed to complain, she worked hard, she was respectful of all adults (even the weird foreign neighbors), and she had a cheerful attitude about life. Of the younger children, she was my favorite to talk with, perhaps in part because she knew a little English and would use it to help me understand her language. She was bright and eager to learn, and had a humility and grace not often seen in children her age.

Menzole had never been to Mombasa. She had only left the village with her mother to visit relatives or buy things at another village nearby, but had never seen the big city or travelled in a vehicle going faster than 10 mph. We were excited when her mother let her come to town with us to buy some groceries one Tuesday.

She spoke very little on the way into Mombasa, taking in the sights and sounds, observing with wide eyes the new places. It wasn't until the return trip, when we were coming nearer to the dusty, bumpy turnoff to our village from the dusty, bumpy road off the tarmac from town that Menzole shared her thoughts of the experience. Staring out the window at the trees we were passing quickly, she turned to me and said excitedly in Duruma, "Look Chiguba, the trees are spinning!"

I looked out the window, and the perspective from the moving car made the trees seem like they were indeed spinning in some ancient tribal dance. In that moment I saw the world with the wide-eyed wonder of a child from Africa, the newness of discovery with no scientific explanation to obscure my vision.

Now whenever I travel, I am looking for spinning trees. Most days I have not forgotten how to see them. And I smile and remember the wisdom and eyes of a little girl in Africa.

CHAPTER 10: BEJA, A FEW BUCKS, AND A 2-YEAR SUPPLY OF COCONUTS

Beja was one of the drunks of the village. Not that he was always drunk, but he was often drinking, which for the Duruma always led to being drunk. There were two kinds of people: Those who drank and those who didn't. Of those who did, there were few if any who could "socially" drink and not get drunk. And there was really only one alcoholic drink for the Duruma people: *Uchi.*

Uchi was palm wine made from the coconut tree. The tips of the young fruit stalks were cut off and tied together so that the sap could be collected in gourds and fermented into an alcoholic beverage. It only took 24 to 48 hours to complete the process, and the *uchi* had to be consumed before the third day or it became almost lethal. A number of deaths in the village related to this drink occurred while we lived there (though a few were of men who started their drinking before descending from the coconut tree and then fell).

The smell of *uchi* was quite distinct from other alcoholic drinks. All the foreigners (and many locals who didn't drink) found the smell very unpleasant. A man (or woman, in the rare case) who had been drinking would carry this pungent odor with them, as it seeped from their pores and sweat. It was quite noticeable even upwind.

Beja was a very friendly man who had two wives. They lived about four houses to the north of us. He had a slight pot belly, perhaps due to his drinking but also due to eating more meat than the average villager. He often walked through the village with his shirt open, carrying a machete he used to cut coconut branches from the trees.

One day after we had been there a few months, Beja's mom got sick and needed to go to the hospital in Kinango. Beja either didn't have the cash on hand or didn't want to spend his own, so he asked to borrow a portion of what he needed for transportation and medicine. I forget the exact amount, but it wasn't more than five or ten dollars. It was a loan, and he promised to pay me back within a week.

After a couple of weeks and no payment, I went to him to ask about the money. "Just a few more days and I will have the money to you," he promised. So I waited a few more days, and again asked him, and again got the same response.

Now, the amount wasn't really that significant. But we had been told by more "experienced" missionaries that Africans in general will always ask for a lot from us, and we were not ones to be always giving unless there was a real need. There is a saying in East Africa that is common among many different tribes:

I almost got a new cow today. I asked my neighbor for his, and he said no.

Indeed most of the Kenyans we encountered were not shy about asking for anything. This was partly due to the poverty that most Africans are intimate with, and partly from their culture of sharing and borrowing. Food, money, clothing (including what we were wearing while walking a trail!), and even our wedding rings were all asked for during our stay. I was also asked many times if I wanted a second wife, but that's another story.

Then one day Beja showed up at our house carrying a bunch of green coconuts. We hadn't asked for them, nor even expressed any liking of them. (Africans drink the juice, which tastes something like a Sprite without the fizz, and they also scrape out the soft white flesh. They are rather refreshing on a hot day, though as with many things I had to get used to the taste.) He said they were a gift. I thanked him, and then in my typical blundering Western way asked about the money he owed me. He again replied, "Just a few more days, and I will bring it to you." In a few more days, he brought more coconuts.

After a few rounds of this, I began to see what was happening. Beja wasn't just paying off his debt with an agricultural product he grew on his own *shamba*; he was cultivating a friendship. He could have easily sold the coconuts from the first few visits to make enough money to pay me back, but then we might not have become friends. Often among the African groups we knew of, one person would become indebted to another solely for the sake of building a relationship. And the debt would likely never be paid off.

We tried at times to pay him for the coconuts, but he would not have it. To him, it was simply part of the relationship he had established. Both green and brown coconuts were in plenty supply in our home, thanks to Beja and the "debt" he owed me.

There is another African saying that relates to this: *We have cows between us.* Beja and I had coconuts between us.

CHAPTER 11: CHILWENGI AND HIS DUKA

Before I left for Kenya, when I need to buy groceries, I jumped in my car and drove to the nearest supermarket. There in a building the size of a football stadium I roamed the aisles to find what I wanted, checking off my list and adding to the cart any items on sale or displayed that caught my eye. I always found what I was looking for, at least in the essentials, and there was always something on sale. For every item, there were many choices in size, price and variety of taste. Someone once counted nearly 300 different types of cereal alone in various sizes, many made by the same company with almost identical ingredients. We love our choices and our convenience.

In Kenya, in the second largest city of Mombasa, there were a few grocery stores. Most were owned by immigrants from India who came over to build the railway in the late 1800s and stayed to become successful shop owners and businessmen. These were small stores, many catering to the Indian population who numbered in the tens of thousands, most with hardly a name to identify the store. And then there was Nakumat.

For the culture-starved missionary or expatriot, Nakumat was a slice of heaven, the closest thing in the country to a Walmart or Target. Granted, it was nothing of the sort, but once you adjusted to living overseas you could find much of what you wanted in that store. Originally a mattress store, the name came from the town Nakuru and the word mattress. Now spread all over Kenya, this store had everything. True, there were not 300 kinds of cereal, but eight is a far cry from none. Even some imported treats could be had for the right price including my favorite, Oreos. When we went into Mombasa, we would usually stop at Nakumat, partly because they had a good selection of items and partly because we needed to see a good selection of items to keep our sanity.

Much more common throughout the country than Nakumat was the local *duka*, which ranged in size from a hole in the wall with two items for sale to a larger hole in the wall with a few more items for sale. The largest might be nearly the size of a one-car garage. The idea of a *duka* was simple: Sell exactly what the guy down the road was selling, for exactly the same price. Most *dukas* would stock the basics for all Kenyans: corn flour, tea, sugar, salt, and some variety of beans. With these simple items, a family could make most of their meals.

Nothing from the store was ever saved at home, and so every day a Duruma mother or one of her children went to the *duka* to buy the daily supplies. The reason the pantry remained bare was due mostly to the fatalistic attitude in the culture. *If I die tonight, I don't want to have wasted any money on food I won't be eating.* After all, an average family really didn't have that much money anyway. Another reason people did not keep much food around was the neighbors. In the Duruma culture, it was bad karma to live better off than your neighbors, even if you actually had more money. To have enough money that you could save up food and supplies for a rainy day made you a rich man, and a rich man too often gets cursed by his jealous neighbors (literally cursed, as in a visit to the witchdoctor). So even if you were rich, you would pretend not to be. In this quasi-Socialistic society, most everyone was kept just above the poverty line, and only a very few prospered.

My friend Hudumu tried to start a *duka* with money I loaned him. He bought a 50-kilo sack of corn flour (called *unga*) and some kilo-size sacks of sugar, and sold them out of his home to the relatives and friends in his village compound. I helped carry a load of sugar on my head, about 50 pounds worth of headache. Of course the items sold and he made a profit, but as so often happens to the poor, he did not get a chance to keep the profits or buy more goods to sell. A relative of his got sick and needed his money to get medicine, and so went his opportunity.

Chilwengi was one of those rare Duruma men who not only had a good head for business, but could keep his head when the pressures of society came knocking. It is one thing to be generous to the poor and to help friends and relatives in their time of need; it was another to lose your only source of income to save face and appear generous to your neighbors.

Chilwengi's *duka* was attached to his home, and his home was just opposite the primary school in our village of Miyani, about a ten minute walk north from our house. He was thus situated in a prime location to sell goods, as students could buy school items they needed, or pick up essentials for the evening meal on their way home from school. This and his good business sense were the keys to his success.

In his *duka* were hundreds of items ranging from the essential to the absurd. Not one but two kinds of *unga*, plus wheat flour and rice, several varieties of beans, canned foods, sweets, pens and pencils and paper, *kangas* for women's clothing, packages of balloons that were as old as I was, bread, several kinds of soap, and the ever important bottles of soda. Soda was most often enjoyed when guests came to share a meal, or at a wedding celebration. Only Coke products were sold all throughout Kenya, and in the local *duka* these bottles were always warm. But after a long hike home after visiting friends, a ten cent bottle of carbonated sugar was quite refreshing, even when tepid.

Next to Chilwengi's *duka* and also owned by him was the only gas-powered mill in the entire area. At harvest time, women from all around would bring their corn to be ground into flour. If a woman could not afford to pay the nominal fee for the service, she could leave some of her corn to be sold later. The texture of machine-ground corn flour was smoother than if done by hand, but some families preferred the taste of home-ground flour.

Chilwengi was a man content to sit and drink a soda with me, and did not require much conversation. I often found it difficult to know what to talk about with Duruma men. I am not chatty by nature, and even less so in a foreign language. We could always talk about the differences between Kenya and America. Sometimes it was difficult to explain some facets of our culture, like the many "boxes" to clean our dishes and wash our clothes and cook our meals. I more often enjoyed asking questions and listening to the revealing of their customs. Even shared silence could still be a comfort.

When I first returned home to America, I was dazzled and overwhelmed by the vast amount of goods for sale at the supermarkets. I had more trouble than usual making a selection (the cereal aisle is still a bit much for me) and for a time would often buy an item simply because it wasn't available in Kenya. I like the great variety and convenience found here, but I very much miss greeting the owner of the store by name whenever I would come. Money cannot buy that convenience, and I would gladly travel to the other side of the world to enjoy it again.

CHAPTER 12: KASSIM WANTS BEANS!

"**K**assim wants beans!"

Hearing Menengala's voice, I looked up from weeding lentils in the little garden beside our house. Her shy five year old sister, Amina, smiled from behind her. On the corner of the porch their youngest brother Kassim was standing, holding in expectation an empty plastic bowl, and looking as much like a whimpering puppy dog as I had ever seen. The sight made me burst out laughing.

In the Duruma culture, the youngest child was spoiled. Always and all the time. It didn't matter if he or she was four weeks old or four years old. The best food, the best clothes, the best toys and time with parents. Boys were spoiled more than girls, but every young child would taste the glory. Until a younger child was born.

The basic idea, or at least what was diffused to our Western minds, was that whatever mistakes were made with previous children could be made better with the baby. The first child taught the parents how to be parents; the process was improved with the second one, and so on. The other factor in this cultural custom was that children, especially boys, were basically the retirement for their parents. When a man or woman had grown old and couldn't work anymore, the sons would take care of them. When women were married, they went to live with their husband's family, often some distance away due to the taboo against marrying someone in the same clan (there were fourteen clans in the tribe). But sons married and lived near their parents, often building a house right next to where they were born.

Kassim was less than two years old when we moved to the village. Emotionally he was the same age when we moved away two years later. He had been the baby for a long time, and it would take a while to grow out of his demeanor, even after a younger brother was born. He was the typical terrible two, and because of his whiny attitude my least favorite of the village children (well, except for the sassy girl who used to stare in our windows until I chased her with a stick, but that's another story). Kassim was spoiled by his mother Mwanajuma and his father Muhammad Badi, our landlord. He was also pampered by his older sisters and brothers, though what they could gain by that pampering I never knew.

Kassim wanted beans, and naturally he thought he should have them. Beans tasted better than cornmeal *ugali* and wild bitter greens like *sukuma weeki*. I could empathize with him, as I had nearly cried during some meals when I was forced to choke down yet another mound of stiff and flavorless *ugali*, paired with all too little sauce to distinguish it from mortar. But something about his look, his way of begging without words, made him almost comical. So I laughed.

I quickly recovered my composure and responded honestly: "I don't have any cooked beans, only dried ones like these." I held up some brown lentils that were almost ready to pick. I knew that Kassim did not have the patience to wait several hours for a pot of beans to cook, and I certainly wasn't going to be the one to cook them for him.

Disappointed, Prince Kassim returned to his house to eat the common lunch of the peasants beneath him. His sad puppy dog eyes became almost tearful, but I also noticed a slight glare in them toward me, as if he knew that I would not play his games. His sisters smiled a bit, perhaps enjoying seeing their brother not getting what he wanted for once. It wasn't my place to teach Kassim manners or respect; he would learn that from his family in time. But neither did I feel bound by the Duruma culture of coddling the youngest child.

I left my weeding, and went into the house, wondering what there was to eat. No refrigerator to store leftovers, no supermarket nearby to restock the food I enjoyed eating, and no familiar foods to eat. Even beans would take nearly an hour in the pressure cooker. The spoiled child in me put on its best sad face and said, "I want beans!"

CHAPTER 13: RECIPE FOR UGALI

Ugali is the staple food of the Duruma, and much of East Africa as well. It is sometimes called *wari*, which means simply "food" in the Duruma language. *Ugali* is made from maize, or field corn, and resembles very stiff mashed potatoes, and also polenta. The flavor is usually nonexistent, though sometimes with home-grown maize it can be slightly nutty or earthy. The texture is rather coarse, sometimes even crunchy depending on how fine the flour was ground. The effect of *ugali* in one's stomach is like a massive lump of dough that tends to stay there for the better part of a day, which may largely be the appeal of it in their daily diet.

The Duruma, for the most part, take to *ugali* like I would eat fresh baked bread, some of them just as happy eating it plain without much sauce. It is good that they like it so much, since they will eat it twice a day on average for their whole lives. Some will even eat it for breakfast, though breakfast will more often be tea with bread or *mandazi*, which are a bit like fried plain doughnuts.

Ugali was always eaten by hand, with the family or guests arranged around a central plate while sitting or lying down on a grass mat. Reaching in with only the right hand and only one person at a time, a piece of *ugali* was then rolled into a ball, and an indentation was made with the thumb. This made the ball something like a spoon to scoop the sauce up with. The trick was to do this without burning the skin off of your fingers, since the *ugali* stayed quite hot on the inside.

I enjoyed teasing my friend Hudumu by trying to dip into the sauce at the same time he did, which caused him to draw back, and I as well. Then when he tried again, I would move forward as well, mirroring his movements until he laughed and scolded me, *"Wey, Chiguba!"*

The most common sauce (*mboga*) was made with greens, freshly found in a nearby field, and very seldom cultivated. Some greens were better tasting than others, but unfortunately one of the most bitter was also one of the most common: *sukuma weeki,* which meant literally "to push every week," or eaten regularly. It and many others were poor man's greens, especially for the poorest of the poor who could never afford to buy ingredients for their sauce. Other greens that were more palatable to my Western taste buds included the leaves and flowers of various squash plants from the garden.

Less often a family would eat beans with their *ugali,* deliciously flavored with coconut milk. Meat was even more rare, though there were always chickens and goats wandering through the village, so I presumed that someone had to eat them from time to time. Meat was usually only consumed when a guest was eating with the family, which did tend to encourage hospitality and the joy of having guests. Even still, it was amazing how far a pound of meat could go when divided among ten people. Women and children did not eat meat as often as the men, nor would they eat choice of pieces when they did, and though this system did not seem fair to me it was one of the lesser inequalities of the African society.

My wife and I ate Duruma traditional food at least once a day, sometimes more. We did this to try and live closer to the people around us and to stretch our somewhat thin budget, but I always craved Western food. I noticed after several weeks of *ugali* and greens that I was losing more weight than I had been from the heat and parasites combined, and I was likewise losing my taste for *ugali,* which had never been much to begin with. Not wanting to waste away any further, we modified our standard lunch to be rice and beans, which somehow satisfied me much more. We also began to eat more meat, which also helped us to hold on to the weight we had. Mostly we ate beef, which could be kept in a pressure cooker for several days if reheated every 24 hours.

Since *ugali* is such a mainstay of the Duruma diet, I thought it would be helpful to include a recipe for homemade *ugali* from start to finish, in case your appetite has been aroused in spite of my warnings. I will assume that you already have a suitable plot of land, probably given to you by your father when you were married (or to your husband from his father if you are a woman). I will also expect that you have a *jembe* or two, which is somewhat like a stout hoe. Only the very rich will be able to hire a tractor to plow their fields. So eat up and enjoy!

Recipe for Homemade *Ugali*

1. Buy seed from the local market a week before the rains are expected to come (if you saved seed from last year and were fortunate enough to still have some after mice and bugs and your own family ate up your supply, then skip to step 2).
2. Wait a little longer for the rain, and hope that it really is enough this year and at the right time.
3. When a wise man in the village begins to plow his land, then you should also. Unless you are wiser than he is. With your spouse and children helping, you should be finished in a few days.
4. Plant your seed in rows, walking on the seeds afterward to press them into the ground.
5. Wait a little longer for the rains to come. Pray to Mulungu to send enough rain.
6. Chase the chickens and birds and the occasional baboon out of your *shamba* until the corn is growing at least a foot tall.
7. A few weeks after the rains come, you will need to weed your field of corn.
8. Weed again every week until the corn is over your head.
9. Talk with your neighbors about the crop this year and whose is doing well.
10. When harvest time draws near, you will probably have to borrow some corn or flour from a family member, since you have used all you saved from the last year.
11. As the corn begins to dry, you can break the stalks to speed up the process.
12. Harvest time: collect the ears of corn in baskets and carry them from the field in the valley to your house.
13. Break the kernels off the cobs and spread the grain out on mats in the sun to dry completely. Chase the chickens away.
14. Pound the grain to remove the husks from the kernels.
15. Winnow the corn to separate the chaff.
16. Dry again. Chase chickens again.
17. Take baskets of grain to the mill to be ground into flour, or if you are poor or particularly traditional you can grind your own flour in your own hand-turned grindstone (two-person models available, inquire

within).

18. Chop firewood and carry many miles on your head.
19. Gather buckets of water from the river or a water hole and carry on your head.
20. Boil this water over a fire in a dark, smoky kitchen (with the firewood you have chopped and the water you carried).
21. Add small amounts of flour, stirring constantly.
22. Make the sauce from greens you have picked, adding tomatoes and onions if you can afford them, and simmering until thoroughly cooked.
23. The *ugali* is finished when it stops bubbling (and it stays in the pot when turned upside down).
24. Shape the *ugali* on a plate, and serve with the *mboga* (sauce).
25. Clean the pot, feed scraps to the chickens and dogs.
26. Repeat steps 19 to 25 twice a day for the rest of your life.
27. Start at the beginning twice a year for the rest of your life.

Now you can cook and eat like the Duruma!

CHAPTER 14: BUCKETS AT THE WATER TANK

Everyone knows that water is essential for all life. This is all the more true in an agrarian society like Kenya, where there are dry seasons without rain for months at a time. The brownness is a blanket that hides all things green and alive, and the dust becomes part of you as you walk on it, breath it, and eat it. Even after a good bath, there is still some grime unwilling to be removed.

Coastal Kenya has two rainy seasons, the "short rains" and the "long rains". These are broken by two long dry seasons. The longer and hotter dry season stretches from November through March, sometimes stealing extra time from April. At the end, every mouth is parched, every water hole dry, and every *shamba* tilled and planted with maize seed in eager expectation of the rain to come. Plant too early and the birds will eat most of the seed; plant too late and the mud can be impossible to dig in. Our neighbor Muhammad prided himself on being one of the early planters who would set the pace for others in the village.

"The rains will come within a week, Chiguba, so we will begin tilling and planting now," he said late in March. I could see only a few empty clouds in the distance, and no real promise of rain.

The heat was misery for us, for all. Not a single living creature had much energy during this time. Even the flies moved slower. And yet all of the normal events of daily life had to go on in spite of the drought. Much of the mid-day was spent in the shade, sitting or lying down on a woven grass mat, talking with neighbors, talking about the coming rain and the coming green.

Of course there was no air conditioning. There was only the mud ceiling, the thick walls, the cement floor, the sea breeze. The night cooled off somewhat, but not enough, and always I missed having a fan blowing on me through the night. It was worse than camping, because when you go camping and sleep in a tent you know that in a day or two you will be back home with all of your creature comforts, and you will remember your time away merely as a fun excursion into the wild.

During the dry seasons, we almost actually enjoyed the weekly trips into town, if only for ice cream and cold soda. Once when we took Muhammad's oldest son, Ndegwa, into town, we bought him some ice cream, thinking it would be the treat of his life. "It burns me!" was all he said about it. He preferred hot tea on a hot day.

Ice was largely unknown in the village. Occasionally a boy from Mombasa or Mazeras would ride the *matatu* through the village and sell flavored ice sticks, something like frozen Kool Aid. Most Africans would not have ice in their drinks, for fear that the cold would make them sick.

Snow was an even more distant concept. Very few of the Duruma even knew what snow was, and they had no word for it except *tilizh*, the Swahili word for ice. None had ever seen snow. When we showed them pictures of our climb up Mount Kilimanjaro and the snow on the "roof of Africa," they were utterly amazed, and some would not believe that such a place was in Africa at all. Not too unlike the explorer clubs in 19th century England who had the same reaction to snow in Africa.

On our home stay with Hudumu and Mbeyu during the first few weeks of living in Kenya, they told us one afternoon that we would all walk to the store and buy *ice*. As it was very hot that day, like most days, we were especially excited about having some ice for our drinking water. We talked all the way down the hill and all the way up the hill about ice and how crazy it was that the Duruma could get ice so far from the big city. The *duka* we were walking to wasn't even on the main dirt road, so it seemed even more wonderful that it would have ice just for us to buy and put in our drinks. That would be worth most any price. When the storeowner measured out a kilo of *rice*, we sadly realized that we had misheard Hudumu using one of the few English words he knew. The 25-minute walk back to their home seemed to take much longer than the first half of the journey.

There was never snow or ice in the lands of the Duruma. The temperature varied from 65 degrees Fahrenheit during the rainy season, to 115 degrees or more in the hottest part of the dry season. And every day no matter the weather, each woman of every household would carry an empty 15-gallon bucket to the water hole (a small muddy pond, really), fill it up, and carry it back to her house balanced on top of her head. The woman could walk in a swaying sort of way, keeping the bucket balanced perfectly on her head, often while carrying a baby or small child slung to her back. The walk from the water hole could be as much as 20 minutes one way. And this was done twice a day at least, to have enough water for bathing and cooking for an entire family. Men did not carry water, unless they were single living alone, which was very rare.

When the water hole was dried up, the women walked down a steep ravine to the river, or what was left of it by the end of the dry season. Mostly just a few muddy pools, but enough to last until the rains came, usually. Bathing and laundry were done at the river on the same trip, to save carrying more water uphill.

We were blessed beyond our awareness in regards to water. Our tin roof had been fitted with gutters by a group from our mission a few weeks before we arrived. Whenever it rained, water from the roof was collected in a 1200-gallon corrugated metal tank. This tank had 15 rungs or bends from top to bottom, looking like stacked rings from a ring toss game. We would usually go through one rung a week during the dry season. Never did it run out completely on us, though several times the tank was down to the last rung. Often Muhammad would come over and rap the tank with his knuckles to find out how much water we had, partly to check up on his adopted white children, and perhaps also to remind us of the differences between us and the people we lived among. Seldom did we need reminding, but humility is never quite a finished work.

When the rains first came, often in a torrent, the tank could fill up in a matter of hours. And when it was full to the brim, water gushed out of a spout at the top. At the first sign of rain, women in our village would rush to bring their buckets to gather the overflow. Rainwater from our tank was much cleaner than what came from the water hole or the river, and it was also much closer. Even before the rain started there would be a line of 10 or even 20 buckets next to our house, often 2 or 3 from the same household, and excited voices talking together. It wouldn't matter what time the rains came, the buckets would be there. And even in the middle of the night, especially with the first rain to overflow the water tank, I would watch from the window or the front porch, having almost as much joy at the abundance of clean water as the women and children gathering it. It was a side blessing of our living in the village, something we did not actively give or do, but that still brought good things to the Duruma.

As with the water tank, our lives overflowed into the Duruma people. But we also went through seasons of drought, of emptiness, of waiting. At these times only a hollow sound came from our hearts nearly empty of joy. We became weary and parched. But the water of life in us was not like earthly waters which dried up so quickly and were gone until the next season. In a moment, as we turned to the One who sent us to live among the Duruma, we would be changed again and filled with a fullness of life, having all that we needed and more. We came so that they might have this abundance in their lives. We poured our hearts into them in the hope that some might drink the water of life.

CHAPTER 15: HARAMBEE FOR THE WATER TAP

Harambee is a Swahili word loosely translated as "togetherness." In reality a *harambee* was a fund-raising event, whether on a small scale as for a student raising money to go to a trade school, or for a larger project like a church or school needing money for a building project. It was a way of sharing the cost and redistributing what little wealth could be accumulated by these people.

The people wanted a water tap, but they would have to raise some of the money to bring the tap to the village. It would be located near the primary school (a 10-minute walk from our house) and would benefit everyone within several kilometers. So a *harambee* would be the answer to raising some of the money.

The usual manner of having a *harambee* was to announce it a few days or a week in advance, to make sure a guest speaker could be there. No refreshments were provided, unless it was at the church where it was combined with a dinner of sorts, or small enough to be at a person's home where tea might be served. People came because it was a social event, a time to get together and talk with neighbors and friends who lived further away, and a time to leave the normal labors of life, if only for a few hours.

When people began gathering, the women would sit in one area, usually on grass mats they had brought. This allowed them to stretch out and for their children to rest or play near them. Seldom would a Duruma adult sit directly on the ground, as a matter of cleanness.

At a larger *harambee,* many chairs would be brought in, primarily for the men but also for some of the women. Women and men sat apart not for any ritual uncleanness if one touched the other, but because they didn't usually converse unless they were related. That being said, several times during our two years I was asked directly by women if I wanted a second wife. One was plenty.

Our long village of Miyani on the ridge was a 30-minute walk from the nearest water tap, which was located to the west along the main road to Mombasa. That tap was basically a faucet with a lock on it that brought water much cleaner than what could be found in the villages. A woman sat by the tap all day, collecting a half shilling or a shilling for each bucket of water. Women who lived close by would get most of their water here, but for the women in our village the walk made it difficult to access the clean water. Imagine carrying 15 gallons of water on your head while walking uphill on a dusty trail and avoiding the occasional rock or thorn or snake. Many of these women would also be walking barefoot.

We were informed of the time for the *harambee* and invited by our landlord Muhammad, who usually told us of any news in the village and made suggestions as to which events we should be a part of. We looked at our budget and decided on how much we could give and set it aside.

When the day of the *harambee* came, we had planned on fasting, not directly connected with the fundraising in any way. At 2:00, we walked down the trail to the school where the *harambee* was being held. There were about 200 people there when we arrived. My wife immediately went to sit by the women, and I went to where the men were sitting. One offered his seat and insisted, so I sat down. Then I was bumped up to a seat closer to Samuel, the elected chief of the village.

That it did not start on time did not surprise me at all, for time moves slower along the Equator. After a wait of more than half an hour, there was a discussion among those who had organized the event. Apparently the guest speaker, a certain man from the school board in Mombasa, had not arrived yet. As I was sitting quietly with my thoughts, my mind dulling a bit from the heat, I was quite shocked when I was asked to be the replacement guest speaker. And only a few minutes to prepare! My first instinct was to decline, but then I asked what I should talk about. The men responded, "Anything you want to."

I had brought my Bible with me in a small canvas field bag. After looking at a few passages pertaining to water I chose one that I could talk about to the people, who were mostly non-Christians.

In the Gospel of John chapter 4, Jesus told the woman at the well:

"Everyone who drinks this water will be thirsty again, but whoever drinks the water I give him will never thirst. Indeed, the water I give him will become in him a spring of water welling up to eternal life."

The son of the school principal, a Christian, offered to translate for me, since I was still learning the Duruma language and also had only a few minutes to prepare my speech. I did intersperse some Duruma, especially *madzi wa maisha,* the water of life. I spoke about the need for clean water and how important this project was, how it benefited everyone. But I was especially pleased to be able to freely speak about my faith in Christ to so many people at once, a captive audience of several hundred as it were. I did not speak for too long, as they might have expected from a guest speaker, but repeated my points so they could carry away some word or phrase of truth.

When it came time to give the donations, the custom was to announce each gift as it was given. Special attention was made of larger donations, and everyone applauded. This had always been uncomfortable for us, but it was just how it was done. Honor and shame were a deep part of their culture, and both played into the announcing of gifts. Knowing your gift would be boldly declared in front of many people might just motivate you to give a little more.

Another interesting thing happened when someone important (like the replacement guest speaker) gave his donation. The amount wasn't told until other people had added some money to it, so that my donation ended up being several hundred shillings more than I had actually given. This was, of course, to make me look even more generous, or else it was a game they played. It was that way for foreigners and locals alike.

When the counting was finished, I was sitting quietly with my thoughts again. The man who had translated for me came up and handed me a piece of paper. On it he had written a verse from the Gospels.

"With the measure you use, it will be measured unto you. A good measure, pressed down and overflowing will be poured into your lap. What you give away, God will give back to you." What a blessing to me, and a reminder to give more of myself and always be willing to let God speak through my life and words.

After the *harambee* there was a dinner of rice pilau, an Indian dish with savory meat and a relish of onions and tomatoes, for all the special guests and "important" people, which we seemed to be included in. I noted that the real guest speaker had shown up toward the end of my speech. I also noticed that even though I had given a Christian talk, Muhammad clung to me afterwards, because now I was someone famous in the village for that day.

The day ended well as we enjoyed the breaking of our fast and meeting new people. I was grateful of the opportunity God had opened up for me to speak, and hoped that some would thirst for the water of life. That hope will remain always, and there will always be work to do among the Duruma, work both spiritual and practical.

When we left the village at the end of our two years there, the water tap project was on hold with no definite start date. The people had raised nearly enough money for their part, but they were dependent on government offices and administration beyond their control or knowledge. To this day I don't know if the water tap ever was completed. But the gift was given, and the words were spoken, and may God yet bring forth the living waters in the hearts of the Duruma.

CHAPTER 16: NOTHING BUT NYOI TO EAT

Everything changes. The seasons fold one into another, and return again. Children grow up, friends grow old and die, new babies are born. Dreams are made and lost and reborn.

Africa is no different. But there, one season or life changes into another that is much the same as before. Change is a force that is overthrown by the monotony of poverty and hardship.

In the West we have seen a significant improvement in the quality of life in the past hundred years. Infant mortality has gone down, the average lifespan has gone up, and there have been great advancements in science and technology.

In rural Africa, except for a few more radios and tennis shoes, life today is nearly the same as it was fifty or a hundred years ago. Most people live from harvest to harvest, from meal to meal. They work hard, very hard, under extreme conditions of weather and often poor health. But their work is not gaining them a better investment portfolio, a nicer house, a newer car. Their work is to survive, to live for another day, and to give their children a chance to survive and live for another day.

At every harvest some corn was saved back to plant in the next season. But often that seed was consumed in the drought months before planting could begin. And even if a family made it that far and planted seed in the ground, there were no assurances of a bountiful harvest. Only hope, which cannot feed your children when they are hungry.

After the seed was sown, there was anxious waiting for the rains to come. Often the birds of the air would steal much of the seed before germination occurred, and the farmer would have to replant, buying seed from his neighbor or else going without and suffering a reduced harvest for it. Sometimes the rains were not enough for a full harvest, or the rain came in torrents and washed away both seed and soil, doing more damage than good. Often they had put literally all they had into the corn growing in their fields.

With the growing corn, all the farms were green and full of hope for the harvest that was to come. Certainly this was the most pleasant time in Kenya, with the weather cooling down to the high 70s or 80s and the dust settling for the most part. The corn was green, the grass was green, the livestock grew fatter, and there was enough water in the water holes for man and beast to enjoy. But the harvest was not in yet.

Even as the new ears of corn were forming, all could be lost to drought or insects. Either plague would mean the plants produced fewer ears of corn, and the ears produced fewer kernels of grain. And this from the already poor red-clay soil of Kenya.

There were two members of the grasshopper family that infested the fields during the weeks leading up to the harvest. The first was the common locust, which could swarm in legendary masses and decimate whole fields in a matter of hours. We never saw this level of destruction, but stories were told of years past when literally everything was lost to the locust.

The other kind of hopper was called *nyoi*. These were deep green in color, the same as the leaves of corn, which made them especially difficult to locate and remove from the plants. They had long, slender bodies with wings folded in a high vertical ridge over their thorax, looking something like a large version of the leaf hopper we see in America. The *nyoi* were less prickly than a locust or grasshopper, making them less uncomfortable to remove from the plants if they could be spotted.

Both the locust and the *nyoi* were edible, but were considered more of a novelty or treat for children than a mainstay of the diet. But they added a good amount of protein to the diet that otherwise consisted primarily of corn meal and *mboga* (sauce or relish), which was often squash leaves and blossoms or locally found greens like *sukuma weeki*. Meat, whether poultry or beef or mutton or goat, was eaten only rarely by the average Duruma family.

A common way to eat locust was to roast them skewered on a stick over a fire, and then to remove the larger legs. This our neighbors did one evening, and brought some to us to sample. I cannot say that I would ever prefer grasshoppers to any other kind of meat any more than the Duruma do, but once you get past the thought of eating an insect, they really aren't too bad. They are very crunchy, and I confess I chewed and swallowed quickly to avoid gagging. But the taste was actually quite pleasant, reminding me of bacon.

We met once a week with a young couple named Hudumu and Mbeyu. We were teaching them the foundations of faith in Christ, in some small way helping the church to stand stronger in doctrine and practice. Like the Duruma farmers, we were often unsure of the future harvest within the church, but we sowed seed in hope and waited patiently just as a farmer must do.

Each week we traded off in whose house we would meet, since the walk between us was nearly an hour. When they came to our house, we tried to treat them to a good meal, especially with meat if we could, since they were a poor family. But we encouraged them to simply treat us as family and not like guests when we ate at their home, so as to not be a burden to them. Sometimes we cooked Western food to see if they liked it. Burritos were quite popular, both with them and with other guests. But pizza, especially with cheese, was almost unpalatable to the Duruma. Laughing, Mbeyu informed us that pizza made Hudumu have *fyoka* (diarrhea), so we never made that for them again.

One day a few weeks before harvest in June, we were visiting Hudumu and Mbeyu. We had brought them a couple of kilos of flour to help with the lunch. We began our teaching lesson, I with Hudumu and my wife with Mbeyu. After some time, Mbeyu told us with great embarrassment that they had no food to feed us, and that they did not know what they would eat for dinner. We were grieved for them, and heartily joined them in fasting through lunch and praying for their provision. I remember reading to them a passage from the Gospels where Jesus teaches us not to worry about where our food will come from, that God would provide all of their needs. The words seemed hollow when the family before us had nothing to eat.

That afternoon, we went with them to their field of corn. Together we collected the green *nyoi* from the corn plants. That would be their meal in the evening, for they and their four children, along with the flour we had brought.

I remember Mbeyu singing a Swahili song from church as she walked through the cornfield gathering *nyoi* to eat. *"Wa milaylay milaylay Mulungu, wa milaylay ni Baraka."* Loosely translated it means, "My God, you are a thousand blessings to me." The seeds of faith sown in her had surely born a great harvest already.

CHAPTER 17: FUJO THE HUNTER

The Duruma used to be much more of a hunter-gatherer people than they are now. Civilization has crept out from the port city of Mombasa, both in influence and in physical space and proximity. The convenience of buying meat already cut up from the butcher, or of buying flour already ground up at the bakery or bread already baked, is certainly attractive to most people in the world when money is available. The Duruma were and are a people living in an uneasy alliance between worlds. Civilization calls to them with convenience and comparison to live at least as well as any other people they meet. On the other hand, the Duruma do not live in a world of tidy asphalt roads and high-rise apartments, but rather in a dusty land still beyond the edges of what the West calls civilization. They do not have the means to buy all of the food they eat, but must grow and gather most of what they consume.

The fact that so few Duruma do hunt and fish is a sign of the changing times they live in. Some work in jobs in the city and only return home once a month. Others spend most of their time as farmers or herders and have little time for what we would call leisure activities. Meat is readily available at the butchery in Kasemeni (a mere 2 hour walk from our village), and many families raise their own chickens, goats, sheep or cattle. Another factor is the decline of forested land and the wild game that live there.

Still, many Duruma men do hunt on occasion, if only for a change of diet or for variety. As my friend Badi once said, "Sometimes a man gets hungry for meat, and he doesn't have money to buy it, so he goes hunting."

The main method of hunting used by the Duruma is bows and arrows. Guns are far too expensive, and also heavily restricted by the Kenyan government, most likely to prevent an uprising by any dissatisfied denizens. Boys often receive a miniature bow and arrow when they are born as a sign of strength and their future manhood, though this toy is worthless for real hunting. When he is a teenager, he will be ready to learn how to hunt and will likely have his own full size bow and arrows.

The bow (*uha*) is carved by hand with a machete (*panga*) from one of three different woods: *mkone, mbwale or mchikoma*, hardwoods with just a bit of flexibility. Normally the *uha* is burnt in the fire or placed above the fire to be made stronger with smoke. Even so, over time it will develop cracks running lengthwise and will need to be bound with a cord to hold it together.

The string is woven from sisal fiber. The succulent leaves similar to a yucca are pulled tightly across a *jembe* to remove the green pulp, leaving only the off-white fibers. Then a handful of these fibers are separated into two groups tied together at one end. Each grouping is twisted clockwise three or four turns, then twisted counter clockwise around the other group of fibers. This is repeated until the whole strand is complete, usually more than a meter in length.

The arrows (*mivi*) require more skill to be made. They are hand carved from *mlanga, mvumo* or *mkone* wood, and like the bow are usually burned or smoked to make them stronger. The arrow is carved slightly thicker at one end to hold the arrowhead. *Kano* (ligament of a cow) is wrapped around both ends to increase the strength and keep it from splitting. The *kano* is first dried in the sun and then chewed until pliable, and it will tighten around the arrow as it dries. Feathers, usually duck but sometimes chicken, guinea fowl or hawk, are tied on with sisal fiber and glued using the sap of a certain cactus. Lastly the arrowhead is glued and tied with sisal fiber. Any used metal will work, and the broken head of a *jembe* is often chosen, filed sharp. Now the arrow is ready for the hunt!

As the Duruma are a social people, they usually hunt in groups. Up to ten or more boys and men will go out during the daytime. Most of the group will make noise and beat the bushes to scare out the game, while one of them will wait ahead. If an animal is shot it may run more than a mile before falling, and the whole group follows. The arrow is retrieved if possible, though it will often be broken by the brush as the animal runs through. The man who makes the kill gets the winners share including the head, hide and choice parts. The rest is divided among the others who helped hunt.

Around our village the game that was hunted included rabbit (*tsungula*), dik dik (*chiphii*), and duikier (*asa*). Dik dik and duikier resemble small deer.

The meat is delicious and the skins are used to make drums. Our neighbor Fujo brought back the leg of a tiny dik dik from a hunt which somehow fed his family and us as well.

Another form of hunting that must be mentioned is the use of a slingshot, called a *panda*. Every boy has one which he uses to shoot at anything, or nothing. Sometimes boys will hunt for doves, or even go into the forest to hunt guinea fowl. But the most common use of the *panda* is to keep hawks away from the chickens. The rubber for the slingshot is bought as a used tire tube, and the ammo is clay balls dried hard in the sun. They are quite accurate at close range.

Fujo the hunter was the teenage son of our landlord Muhammad Badi. His name meant "trouble," but Fujo was less trouble than many teenage sons in the village. He was kind and helpful to his siblings and respectful to adults. He was thin but smiled a lot, which helped give him more substance. He was always generous with what he had, as when he brought us some of the dik dik meat. Another time he had gone searching for wild honey and returned in the afternoon with a bucket full. This was honey straight from the hive, not just with the honeycomb but some of the bees who made the honey as well.

For Fujo, and many others like him among the Duruma, hunting and gathering was in some way an escape from the world between worlds they lived in, a way to go all the way into one of the worlds and so taste life more fully. Perhaps they would not say it so, but simply it was a way to enjoy some rare delicacy that could not be bought in the big city. Sometimes only by leaving what was known could they recapture what was lost and remember who they were as a people.

CHAPTER 18: DRUMS IN THE NIGHT

Dum, dum, dum dum, dum, dum. The drums were beating again, for the third night in a row. A sick woman in the compound down the hill from our house was receiving traditional Duruma medicine, of the spiritual kind.

The Duruma are a people who walk between two worlds, the physical and the spiritual. In reality it is nearly the same path for them, since each world both feeds and devours the other. Physical needs and realities such as food, health, and the weather cause the people to seek out help from the spiritual world, which in turn requires vast amounts of what little income a family has. The cost of an amulet (called a *pingu*) worn around the wrist or neck can be the equivalent of a week's income, and a large ceremony such as one to heal a sick woman can cost many times more. The Western "educated" mind will say that all of this is a waste of money, especially when the cures from a *muganga*, or witchdoctor, essentially amount to snake oil and wishful thinking. But even misguided faith has a place in people, to draw them out of the material world, to look up from the dust and see the skies.

There are two forms of traditional "magic" that the Duruma use. The first and most common is what the *muganga* would use in making charms and amulets and in the ceremonies for healings, exorcisms and rain prayers. The only people who didn't use this magic were the most devout Muslims and the Christians of the Duruma tribe. Nearly every baby born would be given a *pingu* to ward off the evil eye or a wandering demon. The infant would wear this charm until it fell off, usually many months later. Other charms would be hung inside homes to keep unwanted spirits out or to pacify the ones that did come in.

The second form of magic used by the Duruma was known as *utsai*, and the practitioner was called a *mutsai*. This is what we would call black magic, used primarily for cursing another person, whether their health or life or their livestock and crops. This magic was used less frequently than that of the *muganga.* The *mutsai* always lived alone and apart from any village or compound of houses. He was both feared and loathed. Any person who lived alone was thought to be a *mutsai,* whether he practiced magic or not. Sometimes the mistrust led to violence, as when a man in a nearby village suspected of putting curses on his neighbors was dragged out of his house and burned alive in a stack of old rubber tires.

The Duruma people believed in one high god named Mulungu. Mulungu created people to be a sacrifice for himself, and every death is seen as going to feed his guests in heaven. Mulungu is a cruel god, though some benefits can come from him, such as rain or a blessing on crops. The name Mulungu means god, sky or heaven.

A Duruma folktale says that Mulungu sent a chameleon with a message to mankind: "You will live forever." Later Mulungu relented and sent a gecko with a different message, "You will have children, but you will also die." Because the chameleon walked slower, the gecko overtook him and reached man first. The message of death became our reality.

The spirits of the ancestors, even the recently deceased, can intervene for people to Mulungu. If someone has a need, they can give an offering of food or clothing and hope that the ancestor will speak to Mulungu for them. Some graves have a recess in the headstone where the family can put food. The spirits of ancestors are sometimes believed to dwell in baobab trees, and so these are never cut down while the trees are alive.

For the Duruma, life was survival, living from harvest to harvest, hoping for enough rain and enough crops to just get by. Their world was also filled with spirits, mostly evil ones, and their stories were likewise filled with spirits and how to outsmart them, or what happens when you don't.

One of my favorite spirits was the *M'zungu,* or "white man." If someone was possessed by this spirit, they would generally try to dress in a safari outfit (complete with pith helmet) and walk around giving orders to everyone. I say, we're not all *that* bad!

The spirit I remember that disturbed my mind the most was named *Pepo. Pepo* was tall and thin, with a pale face. The weird part about him was his eyes: they were turned sideways so the eyelids closed in a vertical line when he blinked. There were a couple of nights I closed the windows for fear of seeing him stare in at us.

Musical instruments were used in ceremonies to unify the people and to call the spirits needed. The drum, or *ngoma*, was used most often. It had no power in itself, but rather the magic was in the beating of the drum. The largest drum was called *mshondo*, and was about 2 meters long. The sound of this drum could call people (and spirits) from far away.

Another musical instrument was the *kayamba*, which was a flattened instrument of thick woven grass or reeds with seeds inside that gave a rattle sound when shook and thumped in rhythm. The *kayamba* was used in a healing ceremony of the same name. One person informed us that as the *kayamba* was played through a selection of songs, each representing a specific spirit, the sick or possessed woman would react to the song connected to the spirit that afflicted her.

Duruma beliefs about the spiritual world and their responses to it held them in captivity. Rather than set them free, as true faith should, their beliefs were a burden to their lives. There were, of course, the social and emotional benefits of traditions kept. The challenge of the Duruma church was to sift the good from the bad, and incorporate the positive aspects of tradition into worship and teaching. A drum was used at our church, and traditional choruses and rhythms became new ways to sing and praise the Creator. The indigenous church must be a part of the culture, and yet distinct in any area of spiritual contradiction or conflict. This we encouraged and taught, and hoped that God would bring it about in his time and his way.

We as foreigners living among the Duruma were largely unaffected by the magic all around us. Whether it was our belief in God or our disbelief of the magic that kept us safe, we never knew for sure. I am convinced that since we had so many people praying for our safety, surely we were held in the hand of God in a special way during those two years.

CHAPTER 19: THE KAYA

Behind our house to the East was a *kaya*. To the outsider, the *kaya* was just a large long hill covered in dense trees. To the Duruma, it was a holy site, a place that unified the tribe and bound them to their traditions. And a good place to cut firewood if you could get away with it.

The Duruma were part of a group of nine tribes called the *Mijikenda* who believed they originally had migrated several hundred years ago down from what is now Somalia, the horn of Africa. Each tribe speaks a similar dialect, though we found some words could be quite different. The Duruma were the second largest group of these nine tribes, the Digo being the largest. Those two tribes each had over 100,000 people.

Tribal legend tells that when the *Mijikenda* began moving south to settle in eastern Kenya, each tribe carried an idol, a statue of some sort. The idols were so powerful that if the man carrying it let it touch the ground, he would instantly die. Pity the man who got tired on the journey. Eventually when the tribes entered their promised land, the idols were placed on the highest hills in the area, and the place was deemed sacred.

Over time the sacred became ordinary, and the ordinary ruled the daily life. The Duruma neglected their *kaya* and cut down many of the trees for firewood. In the 1980s, the Duruma *kaya* was designated a protected site by the World Wildlife Fund. This status meant that people were restricted in the amount of wood that could be cut from the forest, and a local guardian was appointed – Kazungu, who lived just down the hill from us. Surveys were taken several times a year to ensure that the forest would be preserved as a natural heritage.

Although it was protected, the people still went to the *kaya* to cut firewood, only now they had to make a payment to Kazungu. I never knew for sure if Kazungu was collecting the firewood fee for the WWF or for the tribal elders, of whom he was a member.

The *kaya* was a magical place that called to me. I have always loved trees and wooded areas, and this was certainly part of the attraction. But some of it was the call to the unknown, to be an explorer, to learn and discover the new. I often gazed at the forested hill behind my house, wondering what was at the top. As a foreigner, I was not permitted to go to the sacred site at the top of the *kaya*. My thought was that most of the Duruma had never been to the top, so they didn't even know what they were hiding. Maybe there wasn't even anything left, maybe the idol had long rotted away, or there never was an idol in the first place. I had to know.

"Where are you going, *wazungu?*"

My wife and I were out on a walk, going nowhere. The very idea of just walking without having a destination was completely insane to the Duruma, and they told us so. But we, being Americans, had to have our insanity sometimes.

"We are just walking."

"But where are you going?"

"Nowhere. Can you take us into the *kaya*?"

We were behind our house headed down towards the river between our high hill and the *kaya* when we met a teenager we knew. I asked Khamis if he would take us into the *kaya* and he agreed. After crossing the shallow river and hoping there was no bilharzia or typhoid fever in it, we began climbing straight up the thickly wooded hill to see what we could see.

Khamis told us there were snakes in the woods, but unfortunately we saw none. He told us there were monkeys there too, but we only heard their chatter. Mostly we fought with vines and tangled undergrowth. There were no paths, at least not on the side we chose to ascend. After a long time of fighting the woods and the wild, the *kaya* won the fight. We had made it a third of the way up to the top when we decided to return home. If there had been some kind of path to follow I think we could have made it all the way. I thought I might try another day, but that day never came. Perhaps some things are better left a mystery.

Even now, thousands of miles away and years since I have walked in that land, I think of the *kaya* and dream. I can still see the mist rising from the trees in the early morning. Sometimes in the rainy season fog would settle on the river and in the valleys before the sun burned it away, and the sacred forest would stand out like a green crown upon the land around it. I do not know exactly what the *kaya* means to the average Duruma today, but for me it will always be a place of mystery and peace. Even now it calls to me.

CHAPTER 20: THE BIKE RIDE TO LUTSANGANI

My friend Julius Ndegwa had a bicycle. Well, no, Julius had a friend who had the bicycle. Well, actually, the friend had a brother who worked for a man in town who…no, let me start over. I had a friend named Julius, and Julius had borrowed a bicycle so we could ride to Lutsangani.

My two closest friends in all of Duruma-land were Hudumu and Julius. Hudumu was my disciple and friend, and Julius was my brother and friend. I met with Hudumu once a week or more; I saw Julius almost every day. Hudumu lived an hour away, and Julius was about 4 minutes down the road from me. It also helped that Julius spoke perfect English.

It was Julius who helped me buy my first chickens and rooster (they were named after Muppets characters, the rooster being Gonzo and the broody hen Beaker, but that is another story). It was Julius who tried potato soup and thought it the worst thing he had ever tasted (this from the man who could eat shark meat that had been dried on the beach for a few years). And it was Julius who would call *hodi* late in the evening, when all I could see were his smiling teeth through the screen door.

Julius and I had many deep discussions, often on spiritual topics. He was a strong Christian (in a different church than ours) with a sharp mind. We had brought our Western Christianity (which Western Christians tend to think of as the *whole truth*) which in theory would mesh well with any real Christianity around the world. We did share so much of the basic tenets of the faith, but in practice our worldviews could be quite divergent.

The differences are not so easy to describe, because it is not merely a difference in belief, but in the application of the beliefs and the cultural background from which each person comes to faith. An African and an American can both believe in the same God, both read the same Bible, both sing many of the same songs, and yet retain enormous differences. It is almost impossible to generalize, because even in a single Western denomination there can be great variances of faith and works. And then there are the paradoxes.

In general, the African church is both more conservative and less conservative than the Western church. More so in that they have a greater division between men and women, greater emphasis on propriety and place, greater concern with modesty and restraint. But they are also less formal than us in their expression of worship, for even the most conservative African church knows how to dance. They also have an even stronger family system in general than Evangelical Christianity that makes it easier for their churches to be cohesive. The Western Christian is more of an individual than the African Christian.

I asked my friend Julius once, "What do you do when you need to get away from the crowds and be alone with God, like Jesus did sometimes?" Julius responded back, "You mean when I really need to be alone?" "Yes, how do you get away and be alone?" "Well," Julius replied, "I take two or three good friends and we go for a walk...." I realized then that the Duruma have no real concept of being alone, of being an individual apart from the family or group. This is not better or worse than our individual worldview, it is just different.

The truth is, I learned a lot about what I believed by living among a different people group. Much of what I believed was indeed true Christianity, just as much of what the African church believed was true Christianity. But there are also many beliefs and traditions that are neutral or even opposed to real Christianity that each culture assumes are essential to the faith. When we read the Bible with eyes wide open and attempt to live by it, we can see how far we have yet to travel. True Christianity is something beyond culture, and no one group has cornered the market on it.

One discussion Julius and I had was on clothing, specifically whether women should wear pants or not. His view was from a verse in the Old Testament that says women should not wear men's clothing and vice versa. So I took that same verse and challenged him in return: "The *kikoi* is a Duruma cloth that men traditionally wear wrapped around their waist that looks remarkably like a skirt. Why is that okay?"

"Because the *kikoi* is a man's clothing, and every Duruma person knows that. But women do not wear pants because they are men's clothing."

"But some cultures have clothing for women that looks like pants, like the Chinese," I said. "Who are we to say they are wrong?" Then I pressed him further, "The Bible says we should kiss each other when we meet. Why don't people do that in church here?"

"The Bible doesn't say that, *Chiguba*!"

"It is written at least five times in the New Testament by more than one author to greet one another with a holy kiss," I replied. "So why don't our churches do that?"

"Well, that was for the Jews and the early Church, and not for us today in our cultures," he said. "Sometimes God speaks only to a certain people at a certain time, and something can be right or wrong for them but not for everyone." And then realizing that the same could be true of clothing, he began laughing. "Ah, *Chiguba*, you have me! But I am still not going to greet you with a kiss!"

Julius wanted me to travel with him to visit family in Lutsangani, which was about half a day by bicycle (only slightly less time than if we traveled on foot). Lutsangani was by the sea, or at least near the harbor. We set off from my house in the morning to beat some of the heat, taking the road that went west past the *kaya* behind my house, the forest-covered hill sacred to the Duruma. Julius insisted on pedaling, since I was his guest on the journey. That meant I would sit on the rack on the back of the bike that was intended for books or groceries. I was never sure which of us had the more uncomfortable ride along that dusty, bumpy road.

We coasted downhill, pedaled on the flats, and walked the bike uphill. Truthfully a good portion of our trip was spent walking the bike, which wasn't at all unpleasant compared with sitting on a metal rack and hanging on with all of my strength.

The view was quite stunning along the way. On our right to the south were many different trees growing wild, interspersed with farms and homes, including the En Gedi area where our landlord's second home was at. On our left was a great stretch of valley, mostly farmland, which backed up to the *kaya*. I had always been tempted to climb the *kaya*, even though it was supposedly forbidden for *wazungu* like me.

We stopped at a junction where our road met another, and we would turn left toward the harbor. There at a kiosk I bought sodas for us that had been cooled to a tepid temperature in the shade of the store. They were still much appreciated by two tired travelers. The road now turned mostly to sand, and very soon we dismounted and walked the rest of the way.

His family greeted us warmly, and though they were not expecting me there was easily food and shelter for us. We had brought a mosquito net to sleep under, which was even more necessary this close to the brackish waters where the mangrove trees grew and the mosquitoes thrived. The sandy road to Lutsangani continued straight on into the water, I presume so that the fishermen could more easily carry their catch to market or to home. It was an enjoyable evening sitting near the water, and though I could not see the Indian Ocean from there, I could smell it and hear the waves lapping the shore. There was a lunar eclipse that night.

We returned home the next day, our heads full of greetings to bring to Julius' father and mother and brothers. It must have been a strange sight to see a white man riding on the back rack of a bicycle quite a long ways from anywhere.

Nearer to my home village of *Miyani* I said goodbye to Julius, as he was taking the longer road around to his home, and I wanted to return going as near to the *kaya* as possible. I walked a path I had never been on before, and greeted neighbors I did not know I had. I regret not stopping to have tea with one who invited me, but it was getting late and I feared to walk at night on a path I did not know. I paused under the eaves of the *kaya*, wanting so much to go in and explore, to see what perhaps no white man had seen before. But I looked at the lengthening shadows, and at my watch, and knew that I would have to leave that journey for another day, if ever. I am haunted by paths I did not take, but even more I am deepened by the paths I did take and the memories that I have of those two years. I am grateful.

Chapter 21: Munga the Fisherman

Our house had an equal view to the Southwest of a fertile valley stretching away into the hinterland, and to the Northeast wooded slopes around the river bending toward Mombasa. I greatly enjoyed both views, and both were equally tempting to such an armchair explorer as me.

To the east was the *kaya* which often troubled my dreams, though it would remain elusive to me. I had traveled south of the *kaya* on several occasions, including the long bike ride with my friend Julius to the sea at Lutsangani. And one time I went north of the *kaya* to go fishing.

Munga the fisherman lived behind our house down a trail heading north. He was an older man, probably in his fifties, which was fairly old by Duruma standards. Munga had a son, Bora, who spoke perfect English and was also the most devout Muslim I had met in the entire village. Bora and I had many intense conversations about the differences between our beliefs. We respected each other all the more because we knew what we believed and could defend our beliefs with reason.

One day Bora offered me the chance to go fishing with his father Munga. On the arranged day I arrived at their home in the morning after breakfast. Bora was at school, and Munga was not there.

"He has gone out for the morning," I was told by his wife. "Why didn't he wait for me?" I asked. "He didn't know you would come for sure," was her answer. That was a very Duruma way of looking at life, in fact a very African way of looking at life. Nothing is sure until it is in your hand.

"Should I come back tomorrow?"

"No, he will come back soon, and then you can go fishing with him."

Great, more waiting, I thought. I felt that so much of life was waiting, and it was unfortunately so easy to miss the opportunity at hand because I was waiting for a different one. My American mind thrived on order and a regular schedule. I had to get used to a different rhythm of life in Kenya.

Munga returned after my second cup of tea. He was carrying his net and a paddle he had just carved for his boat. I examined the paddle, very well carved for having been done with a machete. "Munga, would you like me to make a *boka*, a hole in the top of the paddle so you could put a string through it?" Munga wasn't sure about the hole, but seemed to agree so I took out my Swiss Army knife and used the awl to make a hole in the handle of the paddle. Munga was not as pleased as I had hoped, and I began to fear that I had broken some unspoken taboo by messing up his work.

He took me to where he had stretched out his net to dry. He showed me how to mend the net and the knots used to tie it together. I wasn't very fast at the work but enjoyed being able to do something productive. When the net was mended, Munga picked up his paddle and the net and said in Chi-Duruma, "Let's go down to the water and fish now."

We walked about fifteen minutes downhill to the river, and after crossing we walked another 25 minutes along the river to where there was a hut, a few boats and half a dozen men. I recognized one man from my village named Roma, but the other men were strangers to me. After greetings and a brief conversation about the weather, Munga took me to his boat along the bank of the river. The river at this point was more of an estuary, being slow moving, brackish and affected by the tides. The tide was in now and the water was muddy, whereas when the tide was out the mud would be watery. I kept a sharp lookout for snakes of any kind, being ready to make a *boka* with my pocketknife in anything strange that moved. Pleasantly there were no snakes.

Munga's boat was much like a canoe, being wide enough for only one person and just long enough for two if one of them crouched down and promised not to move at all. I crouched down and promised not to move at all.

Munga paddled us out from the shore a bit, away from the mangrove trees on the bank. He held his net over his right shoulder, arranged in just such a way as I can't describe (owing to the fact that I failed in my own attempts to hold it properly that day). Then with a great twist of his body the net was thrown out into deeper water, and the lead weights tied around the edge helped it to sink to the bottom, capturing anything that happened to be under it. Munga pulled the net into the boat, and we had nothing but muddy water on our first try. Again he tried, the net spinning out in a great circle of hope and effort, and this time we caught a small fish. The third time we pulled in a few *kamba*, small shrimp or prawns. Through the morning and past lunch Munga threw his net and gathered what bounty he could from the water.

The bottom of the boat had collected a great variety of fish, only a few of which I recognized, including an eel. Munga sorted the fish, throwing back some that were inedible but none that were too small. Any size fish could be eaten by a person hungry for protein.

I remembered the parable of the nets, where Jesus spoke of the fisherman who sorted the good fish from the bad, signifying God separating the good people from the bad on the Judgment Day. Perhaps God will not be too choosy when his nets are drawn in. Or perhaps like Munga he will find that the catch is much smaller than he would have liked.

I bought a small bag of prawns for the evening meal. For all my intentions of going fishing with Munga again, it never happened. I seldom saw him during the rest of my stay in the village, even when I passed by his home. Munga spent most of his days near the water, casting his net in expectation, and being content with the daily catch. I think that is a great way to live: To work hard to get what you need, and to be content with what you have. And to always have enough hope to cast the net in the water one more time.

CHAPTER 22: ROGERS BEJA AND HIS TWO WIVES

Rogers Beja had two wives. This was permissible in Duruma culture, as a man could have as many wives as he could support, though often even one wife was more than a man could support. Most Duruma homes were a culture of monogamy by default.

A house with two or more wives was a divided house. The husband had to share his time and money with all wives equally, and to provide for each wife separately. Our neighbor and landlord Muhammad did this by having two houses, separated by an hour walk. In this way Dzingo and Mwanajuma rarely ever saw each other until they both lived in the same house, when they saw and heard too much of each other, and we heard too much of them as well.

In the African Inland Church, and most denominations in Kenya, men who had more than one wife were not allowed to serve as pastors or as elders, though they could become deacons. The issue did not seem to come up often, due to the fact that so few men would have more than one wife, and so few people in general were a part of the church.

Rogers Beja was an exceptional man. His wives became Christians before he did, and they won him over by their faith and change in lifestyle, and the courage to step away from traditional beliefs and embrace the new faith in Christ. All three of them were Christian by the time we met them. His wives, Mary and Margaret, began visiting church a couple of months before Rogers Beja. They were at first not warmly welcomed into the church, though not excluded outright. Even the African church struggled with what to do about polygamy.

What I noticed first about this family was the humility and peace that flowed through them. Each of them was quiet and respectful, full of grace and joy. There was no strife or jealousy between the two women, only a peaceful and harmonious relationship based on trust and cooperation. They were sisters in Christ above all else, and there was very little separation between their two households. Each woman cared for the other's children as her own, even nursing the babies of the other wife. Though this seemed strange to us, it was also a tremendous expression of love and compassion.

Many Sundays after the church service, the church body visited different homes, sometimes Duruma and sometimes foreigner. A collection was taken up to help cover the cost of hospitality. Usually *chai* and *mandazi* were served, and we prayed over the household and for neighbors and family to be drawn closer to God. It was a time for us to meet together and be a light in different villages that might only have one or two believers out of a hundred people.

The Sunday that it was Rogers Beja's turn to host the church, several people grumbled (including foreigners), not at the family hosting the gathering, but at the distance we would have to walk to their home. I was quite excited about this visit, since it was close to our home and since we walked such a great distance to get to church each week. Rogers Beja and his wives lived on the same ridge as we did, in our village of Miyani, though closer to the school. So this was about forty-five minutes from the church, uphill most of the way. Still, nearly thirty people came, which was most of the church. This was a testimony as to how well this family had been accepted into the fellowship by that time.

The entrance to their home was lined with bougainvillea bushes, flowering in papery pink blossoms. Not long after we arrived at their home, tea was served to refresh us from the walk in the heat. Afterwards we all were encouraged to stay awhile and relax. Soon trays of chicken and rice were brought out, much to everyone's surprise and enjoyment. Rogers Beja and his wives raised the bar of hospitality by feeding the entire church a meal usually served only on special occasions, when tea and cookies would have been quite acceptable. It was the sacrificial life of Christ lived out in a polygamous family in East Africa, a paradox of truth.

In my time in Kenya, I had to let go of many of my own prejudices and ideas of what I thought was right. Taking the attitude of a learner and a pilgrim, I could sometimes see the world through new eyes, and be renewed in my thinking by the Lord of all cultures and people. "Man looks on the outward appearance, but God looks at the heart." I saw the heart of Christ in a man and his two wives in Kenya.

CHAPTER 23: THE VAN STALLS ON THE LAST DAY

We were leaving the village after two years. We had done what we came to do mostly, and much more in some ways, and we were leaving.

I was ecstatic to be able to see family and friends again, to never have to speak or think in a foreign language, to shop at well-stocked supermarkets with people who looked somewhat more like me, to sleep easy without being concerned about malaria or scorpions or witchdoctor drums in the night. I was dreaming of eating piles of pork and Oreos in rooms filled with ice, ice just to play with and ice to watch melting slowly in the cool air-conditioned room, dripping down my fingers, with a fan blowing on me for good measure.

But we had lived for two years in the village of Miyani on the coast of Kenya. We had become planted in that place, with friends and habits as deep as what we would return to. We had been changed during our two-year tenure. And though we were returning to our homeland, we would never fully belong to any land again.

There is a concept in anthropology that applies equally to missionaries as to anyone who lives in a foreign land for a length of time. As people adapt to a new culture and change their own behavior to better fit in, they sometimes replace old habits with new ones. They can even begin to look on their home culture from an outsider's perspective, choosing to keep some aspects and reject others. Since they no longer belong completely to their first culture, nor could they belong to the new one, they are labeled as third culture people. In some ways, third culture people never quite fit in anyplace, and some will always view themselves as "strangers in a strange land." It is to this that I have come.

As we prepared to leave the village, we realized we had accumulated more than we could bring home, more than we even wanted to. Some things like furniture were too large to bring home, and other items had served their usefulness or were not worth their weight compared with the gifts and trinkets we had picked up in our travels. Most of these items we gave away to certain friends: The *jembe* and our last chicken to Hudumu (this was a nice fat hen from the highlands of Kenya, and her name was Nandi), the file to Fujo (along with my purple shoes), some buckets to Mwanajuma. The furniture was given to a *harambee* to help Julius go to college. The remaining boxes were mostly clothes and odds and ends. These we left near some houses down the path from us, which caused quite a frenzy when a number of families tried to grab it all for themselves.

I bought several stamped and addressed envelopes to give to my friends, to ensure that I would at least get one letter from each of them. Julius, Hudumu, Muhammad our landlord, and pastor Deche from the church each had letters to send to me later. I told them only to write with some news and not just to send greetings, and Hudumu took this to heart. He waited five months to send his letter, and only when he had news of expecting their fifth child, who he would name after me.

On the last day, we gave the remainder of our food items to Muhammad and his two wives to use, along with our last duck and three heads of garlic (plenty to save for later). We were having our last dinner with their family, and we were bringing the food that they would cook. The evening was enjoyable though sad, and the food was delicious. They used all three heads of garlic on the duck though, which was quite potent even for a garlic lover such as me.

The next morning we got up before dawn to leave the village, partly to pick up the other teammates and partly to avoid more sad goodbyes. As I loaded up the team van with our luggage, Muhammad came out to greet me one last time.

My wife went to use the *cho* before we left. Since it was still dark and we had given away our kerosene lanterns, she took the small black flashlight that had been our nighttime companion for those two years. After doing her business, she had the flashlight in one hand and toilet paper in the other. The wrong one made it into the *cho*. I always wanted to bring light to the dark places of the world, but that wasn't quite what I had in mind.

We said *kwa heri* (goodbye) to the dear family of our landlord and friend Muhammad. All ten of his children and both of his wives were on the porch to wave at us. I turned the key, but the van would not start. I tried several times with no luck, so I asked Muhammad and his son Fujo to help push-start the van. We had a sendoff fitting of our time in Kenya, where not everything goes as planned, but there are always people to help you out.

We picked up some of our teammates along the way to the village of Majengo where the church and the team leader's house was. There we said goodbye to the families in the church who had grown along with us in those two years. Most of the team were very happy and excited. I kept quiet and tried to hold back the tears.

At last I stood next to the two men who meant the most to me in the church: Hudumu who I had discipled for more than a year and was like my brother, and pastor Jonathan Deche who had often shepherded me and helped me see into his culture. I embraced them and told them, "*Ana mashi furaha*" – I am not happy.

As we all drove away in the van to catch a bus for the capital Nairobi, the talk was of fun memories in the village, and of what we were going to do first when we arrived home. I could only gaze out the window at the land I was leaving, a land filled with dust and dreams and spinning trees. It will be in my soul forever.

EPILOGUE: WALKING IN A DREAM

YEARS PASSED, RAINS fell, children grew. We lived in Missouri awhile, had three children, moved to Morocco (a place quite different from either Kenya or Missouri, but that's another story). We had an opportunity to travel back to Kenya for a conference, and of course planned a side trip to visit the village and the church, having been away more than seven years.

In our now modern age, Pastor Deche had his own cell phone that he used in rural Kenya. This shouldn't have surprised us but it did, shifting us out of the paradigm that was the village. So we called ahead to let him know we were coming. He lived in a different area, but wanted to see us and promised to be at the church in Majengo on the day we arrived.

We traveled all day from Nairobi to the turn off inland from Mombasa. It was so wonderful to be showing our kids the place where we had lived, to make the stories come alive. On the way we saw a herd of zebra crossing the road, and later we could just see Kilimanjaro's snow-capped peak to the south.

Pulling off of the one-and-a-half lane tarmac highway onto the dusty dirt road that led to Majengo and Miyani, my excitement grew to a frenzy. I watched every turn and bump in the road, remembering so many trips into Mombasa years before. The land seemed unchanged, except for a new bridge to replace one that had washed away. We were returning in February, which was right in the middle of the dry season from November until April. The land was brown except for the tops of the trees.

Being back was like walking in a dream, not one where everything is changed, but a dream of remembering. It was something similar to the *saudade* of the Portuguese, a longing for that which is gone, a reverie. I was blessed to have lived in that land and to return, however brief that return.

As we pulled onto the church property, we saw a large group of Duruma believers gathered to greet us. The women were in one group and the men off together. They were all singing and dancing and shouting with joy. It was a family reunion seven years in the making.

I rushed into the men, greeting and hugging them and squeezing as much Duruma language out of my mouth as I could remember. Some words flowed easily, while other phrases eluded me. The people were all forgiving of my memory lapses.

I found all of the faces familiar to me from the church: Hudumu, Deche, Tsuma, Julius Tsuma, Jira, James Katana, and of the women there were Agnes the pastor's wife, Fatima, another Fatima, Mbeyu, and many others whose names I never knew. All of them had smiles. Most amazing to me was that all of them seemed to be the same age as when we left seven years before. I had expected the people to have aged greatly under the harsh sun and the tireless days of work, but they had a force of youth enough to make me wonder if there was some secret fountain hidden in their land. The only changes in the people were in the children who had grown up, and in some older people who now had white hair. Otherwise, everyone was exactly as I remembered. I wondered if we looked the same in their eyes.

We brought food for a feast with us: rice, tomatoes, onions, spices, and money to buy a goat. Preparations were made and after many hours of cooking, the meal was ready. In Kenya, any meal with rice was special, since rice was not grown locally. Rice pilau was the most loved special meal, imported a hundred years before with the coming of Indians working on the railroad.

By nightfall we were eating rice pilau with goat meat, a taste we hadn't had since leaving Kenya. We pitched a tent next to the church for our family, and most of the men slept in the church on the benches. We stayed up late talking and remembering. I struggled again with having so much, so many opportunities, while most of our friends in Kenya had so little and no real chance for change. There is no way to fully bridge that gap.

The next morning we walked up to our old home on the hill in Miyani. No one knew we were coming, though we suspected a few along the way had heard we were back for a visit. Many people greeted us by our Duruma names, even some people we did not remember. This surprised me at the time, but afterwards I remembered that though we met and knew many of the Duruma people, we were among the very few foreigners to have lived near them, and so were known to most of them.

The children of Muhammad Badi, our former landlord, greeted us warmly when we arrived. His family was now living in both of the houses on the hill, and they prepared a room for us to sleep in that night (our former kitchen). Mwanajuma made a chicken dinner, and we waited for Muhammad to return from a journey he had made. All of the children had grown up and were mature and reserved. In my mind's eye they were still little children, unaged by the years. A few of the kids who were very young when we left, like Kasim and Mwamzandi, were uncertain how to talk with us. They did take our stories and teasing with a smile though.

At last Muhammad arrived just before dusk and out of breath. He had been at a school meeting in a town 12 miles away, and had walked back at a brisk pace once he heard we were at his home. He also looked unchanged, except for his hair which was turning gray. It was good to be back in our Duruma family, with Muhammad still like a father figure to us, and his children as our own.

As for our three kids, they adapted quickly to their cultural immersion. They played with other kids and climbed trees and dug in the dirt just like Duruma children do, and hardly complained about the things they didn't have or the strange taste of the food. Our Duruma friends were proud that we were able to have children (they were worried about us when in our third year of marriage we were still childless).

The next morning we walked back to the church in Majengo. Mwanajuma walked most of the way with us, showing the respect and friendship that was still strong after all those years. We caught a *matatu* back to Mombasa where we would take the bus going to Nairobi.

It was sad to leave again, but less so than our first leaving. I knew when I left the first time that I had to come back at least once in my lifetime, and now I felt complete. I knew my heart would always be connected to that dusty place and those beautiful people, and for all the miles between us there would be no distance in our hearts.

GLOSSARY OF DURUMA AND SWAHILI WORDS

Asante Thank you (*nashakuru* in Duruma)

Bado Not yet

Banda A building, usually temporary, consisting of a roof with supports

Basi Enough

Bwana Sir (or Lord if used of God)

Chai Tea, usually made with milk and sugar and sometimes flavored with cardamom

Cho A toilet, especially of the non-plumbing type (thought to be a home of unclean spirits, but more often unclean gases)

Duka A small store ranging in size from a few square feet to a small house, and selling anywhere from 1 to 1,000 items

Hapana No

Harambee A fundraising event, sometimes including an auction

Hodi Greeting call to get someone's attention or know if anyone was at home

Jambo Hello

Jembe A hoe, thicker and wider than the Western variety

Kamba Shrimp or prawns

Kanga Cloth worn as a skirt or shawl by African women, printed in various bright colors

Kaya Holy ground, usually a wooded hilltop

Kikoi Cloth worn by men essentially as a wrap

Kuku Chicken, alive or cooked

Kwa Heri Goodbye

Lamkadze Morning greeting

Madzi Water

Mandazi Fried doughnut, less sweet than American, made with wheat flour (unga wa ngano); also called *mahamore*

Matatu A bus, or more often a van, used to transport people between towns and around larger cities; always packed full and with interesting names like "Bouncin Wit Da Hom Boyz" painted on the side

Matsere Corn or maize plants or seeds

Mboga Sauce or relish, usually greens, served with *ugali*

Mbuzi Goat, or goat meat

Mijikenda The group of 9 tribes including the Duruma and Digo who live in East Kenya

Mimi Me

Muganga Witchdoctor or healer

Muhi Tree (plural *mihi*)

Mulungu The high god in Duruma theology; also sky or heaven

Mutsai Witchdoctor who uses black magic (*utsai*) or curses

Mwana Child

Mzungu A foreign or white person (plural *wazungu*)

Ndiyo Yes

Ngoma Drum

Ngombe Cow

Phanga Any variety of falcon or hawk, stealer of young chickens and ducks

Panda A slingshot

Panga A machete

Peramende Candy or sweets of any kind

Pingu A charm or amulet worn as a bracelet or necklace to ward off evil spirits

Shamba A cultivated field or garden

Sindadze Afternoon or evening greeting

Uchi Alcoholic drink made of coconut palm sap fermented directly from the tree

Ugali The primary food of the Duruma and many others in East Africa, made of boiled maize flour and having the consistency of stiff mashed potatoes (also called *wari*)

Uka Go away! (often told to dogs and chickens, both of which seem to understand)

Unga Flour made of maize
Utsai Black magic or curses
Wazungu Plural of *mzungu*
Wendaphi Where are you going?

About the author

I live in Kansas City where I was born and raised. I enjoy time with my family, cooking and eating, gardening, reading and writing, fly fishing, playing Celtic music, being outdoors, and learning about the world around me. I am studying Irish and hoping for better luck than the last seven languages I have attempted. I still dream of places I have walked, and the path leads further up and further in.

By the same author

Glacial Dreams
A Paradox of Shadows
The DRWN Trilogy (coming soon)
https://www.smashwords.com/profile/view/Spinningtrees (my main page on Smashwords, with links to download my free poetry books and where new books will be released)
http://thetreeswerespinning.tumblr.com/ (photos of Kenya and my Duruma friends)
"If I were to fly away on the wings of the dawn, and settle down on the other side of the sea, even there your hand would guide me…." Psalm 139

www.ingramcontent.com/pod-product-compliance
Lightning Source LLC
Chambersburg PA
CBHW021334160726